The Best Of *The Mailbox*®
Arts & Crafts

W9-CLW-107

A collection of art activities
from *The Mailbox*® magazine

Compiled by:
Stephen Levy
Ada Hamrick

Copy editor:
Gina Sutphin

Artists:
Jennifer T. Bennett
Cathy Spangler Bruce
Donna Teal

Cover design:
Jennifer T. Bennett

Table Of Contents

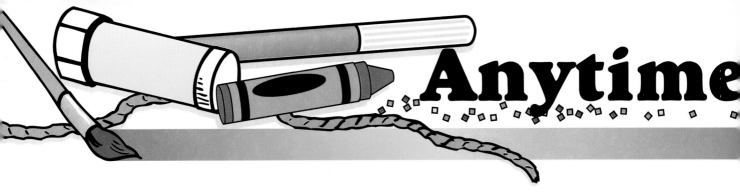

Anytime

- Adapt ideas in this book to go with a particular season, holiday, or theme. For example, adapt the "Winsome Wind Sock" activity on page 17 for different holidays such as Thanksgiving or Christmas.

- Get parents and students involved in helping you collect art supplies from home. Duplicate the reproducible letter on page 4 to send home at the beginning of the year. Before duplicating, place a check beside items you will need for your art program and add your signature.

- Don't have time each week for a whole-class art lesson? Many of the ideas in this book are very simple and perfect for independent projects. Place supplies and instructions at an art center. Assign several students to be your art helpers. Rather than interrupt you while you are working with groups, students can take their questions about the art center activity to one of the special helpers. Don't forget to recognize your special helpers with the reproducible awards on page 5.

- Have you ever wanted to do a classroom art activity, but you didn't have enough of one item? Put a sample of the needed item and the number you want on a Wanted Sign outside your door. Post a daily count of how many you have collected to avoid an overflow.

- Check at your local printing shop for leftover and scrap paper available for teachers. You'll probably find pieces in all colors, sizes, and weights. Stock up on large and small scraps to make flash cards and games as well as art projects.

- Install a cafe curtain rod as a dispenser for a big roll of shelf or freezer paper in your art center. Hang a pair of blunt-nosed scissors nearby so that children can help themselves.

- To make chalk art pieces easier to work with, dip chalk into sugared water before drawing. Finished art will not smear.

- Make paint containers large enough for several students to use. Cut plastic milk containers (half-gallon or gallon) about two inches from the bottom. To reuse, simply rinse them out.

Art Tips

- Is a squirt of tempera paint all you need? Save plastic, squirt-top, liquid detergent bottles. Mix tempera paints at the beginning of the year, and store them in these clean bottles. You'll save time when paint is needed for art projects or small touch-ups.

- Don't throw away old brushes from fingernail polish bottles. Clean them in nail polish remover and use as paintbrushes for those hard-to-reach places.

- Here's another use for old fingernail polish bottles. Use empty ones to store glue. The small brush prevents children from getting too much glue on their projects, and that saves on your glue!

- Clean up sloppy painting times with empty roll-on deodorant bottles. Fill with thinned tempera paint and use on large pieces of paper. Remind the children to shake the bottles often—with the caps on!

- Plastic, six-pack drink holders make great mobiles. Tie a string to each ring and attach your pictures. They're much softer and lighter than coat hangers.

- Keep a can of laundry soap flakes by the sink for easy washup after art activities. Instruct children to place one finger in the flakes before washing. It takes less time and less soap, and results in less mess.

- An easy way to get those dirty worktables clean is to let children finger-paint on the tabletops with shaving cream. They'll have loads of fun, the tables will be clean, and the room will have a good, fresh smell.

- Wipe out sticky hands during activities requiring glue. Keep a damp sponge at each worktable to clean messy hands. This technique eliminates disruptive traffic to and from the sink.

- Use monofilament fishing line under the chalkboard for displaying artwork. Run the line through the center springs of short, colored clothespins to have a handy way to hold up work.

- To display children's artwork, cover three boxes of graduated size with fabric or Con-Tact® paper. Stack the boxes; then staple flat artwork to the sides. Use the top of the pyramid for three-dimensional artwork.

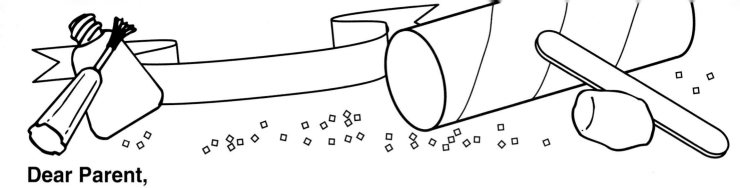

Dear Parent,

Can you help us? Our class needs the art supplies indicated below. Please send any available materials to school with your child.

_____ egg cartons	_____ Styrofoam® meat trays
_____ pipe cleaners	_____ fabric scraps
_____ empty nail polish bottles	_____ newspapers
_____ cotton balls	_____ yarn
_____ ribbon	_____ sponges
_____ wallpaper samples	_____ glitter
_____ buttons	_____ paper plates
_____ empty liquid detergent bottles	_____ tubes from paper towels,
_____ sandpaper	toilet tissue, gift wrap
_____ baby food jars	_____ ice-cream sticks
_____ gift wrap	_____ old greeting cards
_____ paper towels	_____ paper or plastic bags
_____ empty plastic milk containers	_____ empty plastic liter bottles
_____ plastic drinking straws	_____ plastic wrap
_____ old magazines or catalogs	_____ aluminum foil
_____ clothespins	_____ waxed paper

Other: _____

_____

Thank you!

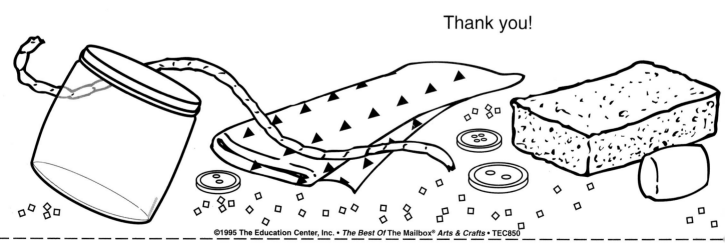

Note To Teacher: Before duplicating, check the items you need, add any others not on the list, and sign your name. Send home with students at the beginning of the year or any time supplies are needed.

There's nothing like

an *original* by

_____
name

_____
name

_____
date

Very Creative Artwork!

Back-To-School Banners

Weave these personalized banners into your back-to-school festivities! To begin, fold a 12" x 18" sheet of construction paper in half, widthwise. Use your ruler to draw a faint line approximately 1 1/2 inches from the open end; then cut a series of 1 1/2-inch-wide wavy lines from the fold to the pencil line. Unfold the resulting loom and set it aside. Next draw a set of 1 1/2-inch wide wavy lines across the width of another 12" x 18" sheet of construction paper. Number the strips and cut them apart. Then tightly weave the strips through the loom in order. On the last strip that will fit in the loom, trim one side to a straight edge. (See the illustration.) Discard the extra strips and glue the ends of each woven strip in place. To personalize the banner, trace and cut out the letters needed from a third color of construction paper. Glue the letters in a pleasing arrangement on the woven banner.

Precious Puppets

Simple and sweet, these colorful critters make perfect puppets. To begin, draw a circle near the center of a ten-inch square of white construction paper. Then, using a variety of colors, draw a series of rings around the circle. Each ring should be slightly larger than the one drawn before it. Continue in this manner until the paper is nearly filled; then draw ears near the top of the circle. Using a black crayon, add desired facial features; then cut out the shape. Tape a pencil to the back of the cutout to complete the project. The resulting puppets will be as unique as your youngsters. For a fun get-acquainted activity, have each puppet share three things about its owner!

Split Personalities

Help students gain confidence in their drawing ability with this easy and fun project. Have each child cut out a large, close-up picture of a face from a magazine. (Be sure the person is facing forward.) Have the student fold the picture in half and cut it down the middle. After gluing one half to a piece of white construction paper, he draws and colors the other side of the face, using the remaining half as a guide. To finish the project, have students cut out and glue construction-paper frames on top of their drawings, trimming the edges. Mount the framed masterpieces on a bulletin board entitled "Split Personalities."

Name Designs

Start off the new school year with a bright bang of color! Begin by giving each student a large piece of white construction paper. Instruct students to completely color in their papers with unique designs. Next have each student print his first name on another sheet of white construction paper. With crayons, the student outlines his name several times, then colors in the resulting spaces with more bright colors. Finally the student cuts out his name and glues it onto his full-page design.

Nature Mobiles

The first month back at school is a great time to introduce a unit on plants. Follow up your study by having students create nature mobiles. First have students collect interestingly shaped sticks, twigs, or vines on which to suspend their nature objects. (If desired, use coat hangers for frames instead.) Then have students gather items such as pinecones, seed pods, milkweed pods, dried weed plant parts, driftwood, and colorful pressed leaves.

When all materials have been gathered, take the class to the gymnasium. Provide a supply of thread or thin wire, scissors, and a hot glue gun. Also place broomsticks between ladders to create rods on which students can hang their mobiles while they work. Parents may assist students as they construct their mobiles. The finished mobiles are hung from the ceiling of your classroom, just in time for Open House!

Apple Prints

This time of year, apple prints pop up everywhere. But here's a timesaving variation on a tried-and-true theme. Cut an apple in half horizontally. Press one half onto a red ink pad and the other onto a green ink pad. Alternately press these two apple-half "stamps" to decorate a sheet of art paper. The mess is kept to a minimum, and you'll love the transparent quality of the prints.

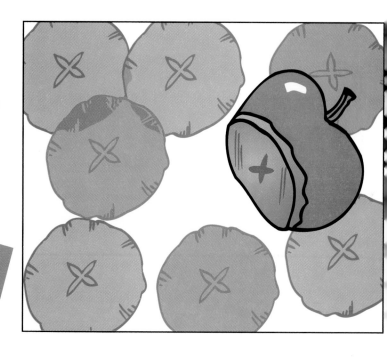

Shapes With Charisma

Pipe cleaners aside, no one will get bent out of shape over this art activity. Tape four pipe cleaners to a poster-board shape for arms and legs. For feet and hands, tape small versions of the same shape to the unattached ends of the pipe cleaners. Add wiggle eyes or pom-pom eyes, before drawing other facial features with a black marker. Attach tufts of fake fur, crumpled tissue-paper strips, or curling ribbon for hair, if desired. Bend the pipe cleaners to pose your irresistible shape creature.

People Cutouts

Here's a simple way that little ones can make cutouts of people. Fold a 6" x 9" sheet of construction paper in half. Trace a ruler onto the paper as shown. Cut along the lines, saving the scraps. Unfold the upside-down *v*-shaped piece. This will be the torso and legs of a person. Using the pieces from above the ruler lines, trim the points away as shown and glue them to the back of the torso for arms. Add a round head cutout with features, as well as hands, shoes, and things for the person to hold. Fold the arms forward to create different positions. By varying colors, details, and objects held, a child can turn this basic figure into anyone from a drummer to an astronaut.

Familiar Faces

Here's a fun-filled project for that first week back at school! Have each student roll a 12" x 18" sheet of construction paper into a cylinder, taping the edges together. Challenge students to turn their cylinders into replicas of themselves! Demonstrate how to cut paper strips in various lengths and curl them with a pair of scissors. After gluing the hair in place, have students add other features using scraps of construction paper, fabric, wallpaper, tissue paper, and other materials. Encourage the use of 3-D elements such as ears that stick out. For fun, set the finished projects out on a table for Open House and have parents try to guess their identities!

Personality-Strip Mobiles

With just a few simple materials, your students can create interesting back-to-school mobiles.

Steps:

1. Fold a 12" x 18" piece of construction paper in half lengthwise; then cut on the fold and glue the ends together to make one long strip.
2. Lightly draw a design that runs the length of the strip.
3. Write your name somewhere within the design.
4. Clip words or phrases that describe your personality from old magazines. Glue these words onto the strip.
5. Make cuts every 1/4" on both of the long edges of the strip, stopping when you reach the design's lines.
6. Fold the cut strips to the front and back, alternating as you work.
7. Punch a hole in the top of your strip, add a length of colorful yarn, and hang.

If students want to add more color to their strips, have them use a hole puncher to punch out dots from various colors of paper. Students glue the dots on the mobiles before folding the cut strips.

Back To School

Put Your Best Foot Forward!

Step right up to a great back-to-school art activity! Have each child rub one sneaker-clad foot on a dusty hallway or playground, and step firmly onto a 9" x 12" sheet of white construction paper. (Students who aren't wearing sneakers or who don't have much of a pattern on their shoe soles can ask a classmate for a print.) The student outlines the resulting dusty print with a black crayon or markers; then he uses brightly colored markers or crayons to color in the outlined areas. Have students cut out their sneaker prints and mount them on black paper for a display that's got lots of "sole"!

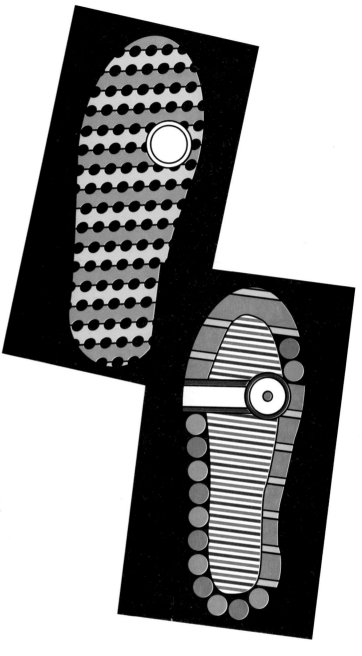

Name Banners

What's in a name? An interesting design, when your students complete these eye-catching projects! Have each student use a pencil and ruler to divide a 12" x 18" sheet of white construction paper into at least 14 squares and rectangles. Have the student go over his pencil lines with one color of marker. The child then uses markers to write one letter of his name in each section, randomly skipping sections to create an interesting design. After coloring in the boxes containing letters, the student fills the remaining boxes with designs or pictures which describe his personality, talents, hobbies, etc. As a finishing touch, have students add construction-paper fringe to the tops and bottoms of their papers to create banners that are ready to proudly display!

Classroom Banners

Create a unique banner to display in your classroom from the first day of school until the last. To make the banner, hem the edges of one-fourth of an old white sheet. Have each student use crayons to decorate a 6" x 6" piece of fine-grain sandpaper with his initials or simple pictures to illustrate hobbies, favorites, etc. (Be sure that students color heavily and write their initials backwards.) Arrange finished pieces facedown on the banner and press with a protected iron until the crayon wax melts. Protect your ironing surface with several layers of newspaper. On the last day of school, cut apart the banner and return the sections to your students since your year of "hanging around together" is over!

Patchwork Names

The first day of school is the perfect time for this simple, yet striking, art project. Give each child an 8 1/2" x 11" piece of ditto paper. Have the student lightly draw a grid on his paper to divide it into one-inch squares. Starting in the upper left-hand corner, the student fills in each square with one letter of his first name. He continues until all of the squares are filled in. (Tell students not to worry if the last set of letters doesn't spell out the entire first name.) Encourage the use of "fat" letters as shown. Finally have students color in the squares, repeating color patterns for identical letters. When finished designs are attached to a wall or bulletin board so that they touch each other, they form an eye-catching patchwork quilt.

Doorknob Hangers

Start your students off to a year of good study habits with this art project. For each student, duplicate the pattern onto white construction paper. Have students personalize their hangers with crayons or markers. Glue each hanger onto a colorful piece of construction paper and cut it out, leaving a border around the edges. Laminate; then cut out the circular section at the top. Students slip the hangers over their doorknobs when studying to prevent disturbances. (If the doorknob is too big, cut a slit at the top as shown.)

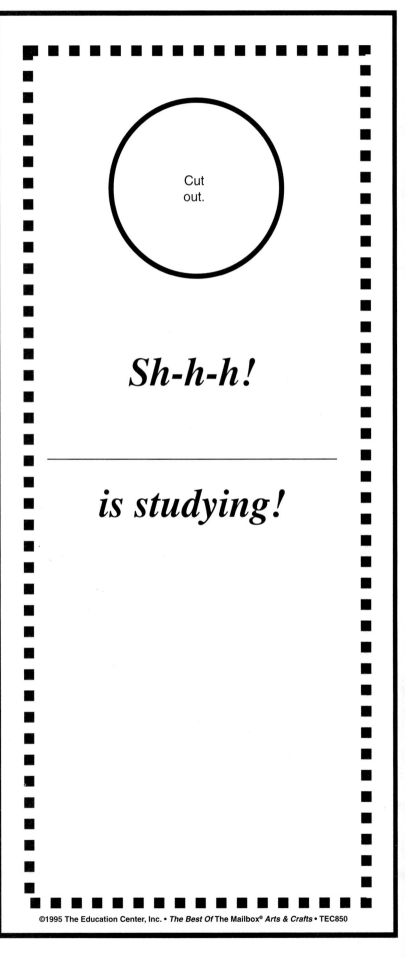

Cut out.

Sh-h-h!

is studying!

Glub, Glub

Before the beach umbrellas are stored away, there's just enough time for an underwater art splash. To make one of these pictures, thoroughly wet a large sheet of art paper in water. Paint the paper with several colors of watercolor paint, allowing the colors to bleed and blend. Onto the wet paper, toss a few grains of salt. The following day, cut simple fish shapes from the painted paper. Also cut several circles for bubbles. Arrange the shapes on a dark blue construction-paper or tagboard background. If you have paper left over, add a bit of coral, seaweed, or more fish to the scene. Use a black marker to add a few details.

Personalized Spirals

Help students get acquainted with this three-dimensional art project. Using a coffee can lid, have each student trace a circle onto colorful construction paper. Starting on the outside edge, the child cuts the circle into a spiral. Have students cut different shapes (with tabs) out of construction paper and label them with hobbies and interests. Students glue the labeled shapes onto the spirals by the tabs and fold as shown. Have students share the information on their spirals with classmates. Hang spirals from the ceiling to display.

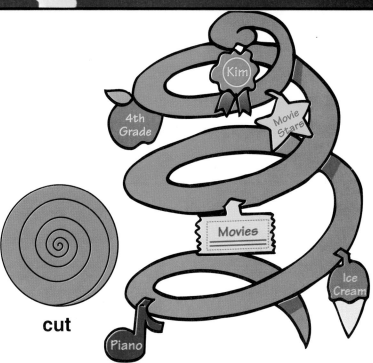

cut

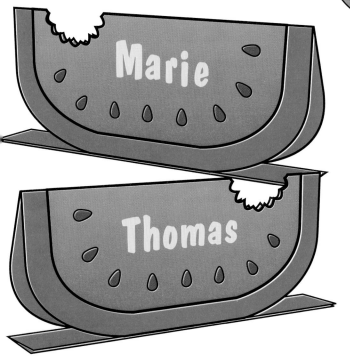

Mouthwatering Nametags

These tasteful three-dimensional nametags are hard to overlook! Using the pattern on page 14, make two tagboard tracers: one of the entire pattern and one of the center portion only. To make a nametag, fold in half a 9" x 12" sheet of green construction paper and an eight-inch square of red construction paper. Trace the larger pattern on the green paper and the smaller pattern on the red paper. Cut on the resulting outlines. Next sandwich the green cutout between the red cutout by aligning the fold and cut lines; then glue the two together. Personalize and decorate both sides of the project. To complete the project, fold the tabs inward and glue one tab atop the other. When the glue is dry, adjust the folds as needed so that the resulting nametag is freestanding. Tape each student's nametag to his desk.

Pattern

Use with "Mouthwatering Nametags" on page 13.

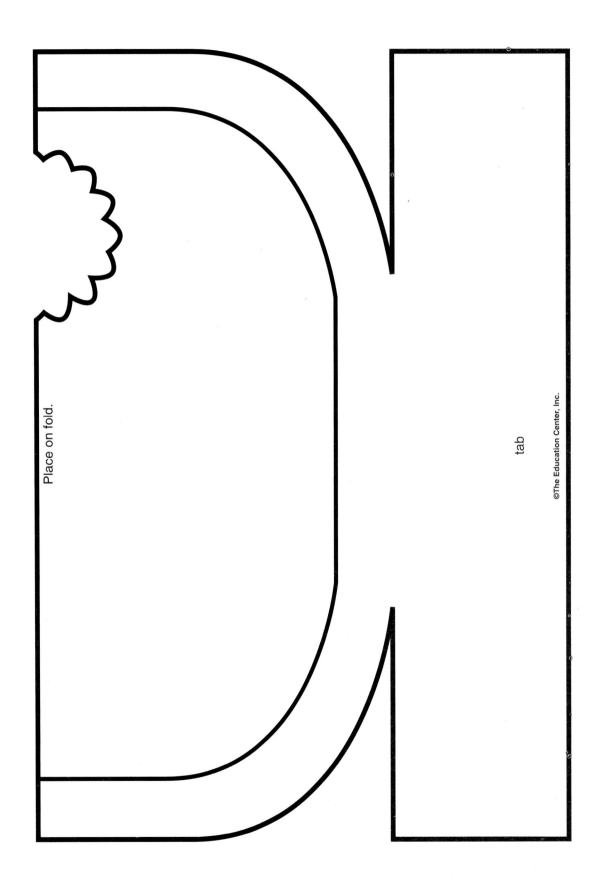

Place on fold.

tab

©The Education Center, Inc.

Eagle Art

Whether you use this activity to raise your students' consciousness about the endangered status of our national bird or to fascinate your youngsters with a bit of seasonal historical trivia (Ben Franklin wanted the turkey—rather than the eagle—as our national bird), it will be a hit. Cover a 12" x 18" tagboard rectangle with aluminum foil. Duplicate or trace the eagle pattern (page 16) onto brown construction paper. Cut out the eagle; then cover it with balled-up squares of brown, white, and yellow tissue paper which have been dipped in glue. When dry, glue the eagle atop the foil-covered rectangle. To complete the patriotic effect, add foil stars and strips of red-white-and-blue ribbon or bulletin-board border.

Create A Creature

In just one fun art period, you can fill your class with a collection of creative creatures! Divide your art period into three equal sections. Tell students that when one-third of the period is over, they must be finished with that step. Give each child a strip of computer paper made up of three sheets. Each student folds his paper so that only one sheet is showing. On that sheet, he draws and colors a creature's head **only**. When time is up, the student draws lines extending onto the middle sheet to show where the neck should continue. He then folds his paper so that the head is hidden and the middle sheet is faceup. Have the students exchange papers. Without looking at the head, the student draws a body onto the middle sheet. At the end of the time limit, the student draws lines onto the third sheet to show where the legs or tail should begin. Papers are folded and exchanged again with a third person who finishes the creature.

After the drawings are done, unveil the creatures! Extend the activity by having students write about their fantastic creatures.

Pattern

Use with "Eagle Art" on page 15.

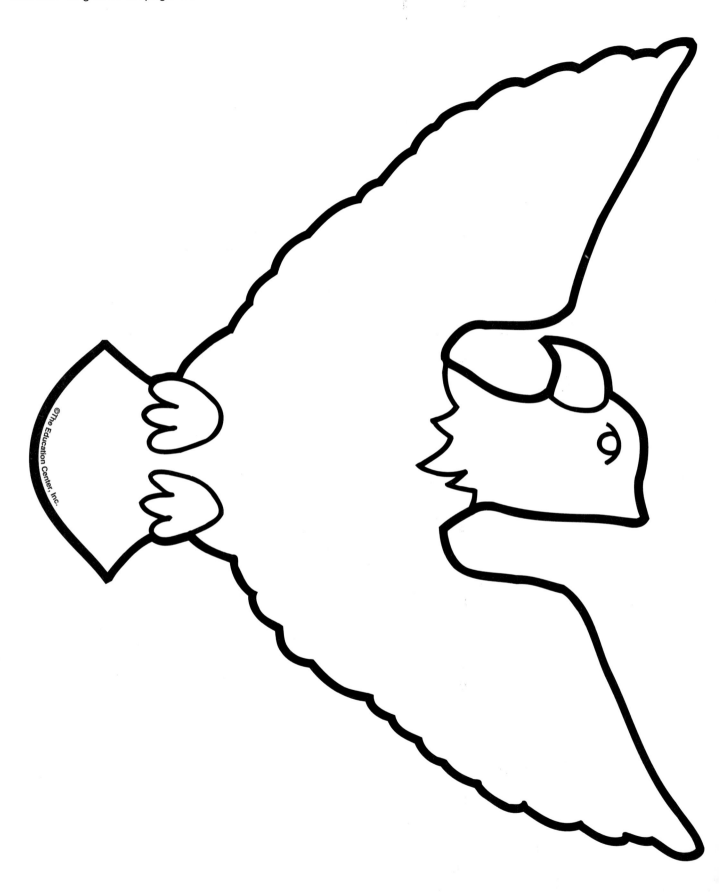

Grandparents Day Surprise

Grandma's definitely going to get attached to this refrigerator magnet! Begin by tracing a juice can lid onto brightly colored paper. Cut the circle slightly smaller than the outline, and glue it inside the rim of the lid. To this colorful background, attach a photo or a bit of artwork. Glue lace or other edging around the rim of the lid and add a tiny bow if desired. Attach a self-adhesive magnet strip to the back of the lid to complete the project.

Winsome Wind Sock

Stirring in gentle fall breezes, these student-made patterning projects will add a touch of festivity to the air. Using holiday stamps, stickers, or original renderings, design a pattern (or repeat one) on a 3" x 18" strip of white construction paper. Glue the strip atop an orange one measuring 6" x 18". Place facedown. Spread glue lightly along the lower edge. To form a repeated color pattern, attach 1" x 14" tissue-paper strips atop the glue. When the glue is dry, staple the strip's ends together, punch holes near the top for hanging, and suspend from the ceiling using yarn.

This time of year, there's a holiday around every corner. Adapt this idea for Thanksgiving, Hanukkah, Christmas, or New Year's Day.

Fall

Corn Mosaics

With a kernel of an idea and a kettle full of kernels, your youngsters can create eye-catching mosaics. Prior to this art project, spray kernels of popcorn several different colors. Allow the kernels to dry. Fill each section of a muffin tin with a different color of kernels. On a poster-board square, draw a simple design. Select and glue kernels to the design. Allow for drying time.

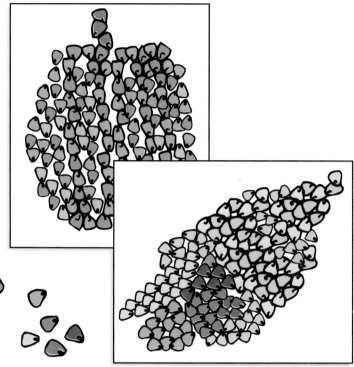

Legendary Blossoms

Share a Native American legend with your youngsters, and when these blossoms appear they'll be tempted to pass the story on. Set the mood for this project by reading aloud *The Legend Of The Indian Paintbrush* retold and illustrated by Tomie dePaola. To make an imitation Indian paintbrush, roll a sheet of red or orange paper from a narrow side. (Use fluorescent colors if they're available.) Holding the lower part of the roll securely, flatten the upper 1/3 of the roll. Using sharp scissors, cut down the center of the flattened portion. Reflatten the upper 1/3 of the roll so that the cut edges are at the sides. Make another cut down the center of the flattened portion. Holding the uncut roll end, gently pull an inner piece of the cut paper, allowing the petals to emerge. Tape near the uncut end. Create a stem and leaves by rolling green paper in the same manner, but allow the roll to be a bit wider than before. Cut, pull, and tape as before. Slide the taped end of the bloom into the leafy section. Make several flowers in this manner.

To display these bright flowers, trim away the upper 1/3 of a medium-size brown paper bag. Roll the top of the bag down. Flatten the bag; then use watercolor markers to decorate the front panel. Secure the flowers in the bag by using crumpled newspaper or tissue paper.

1st cut

2nd cut

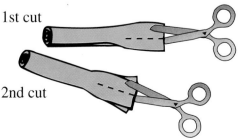

Autumn Mosaics

Turn Styrofoam® meat trays into colorful fall projects! Ask each child to bring in a shallow box or lid and several cleaned, white, Styrofoam meat trays. Follow these steps:

Steps:

1. Paint the inside of a box lid with a dark color such as black, dark blue, or purple. Let the lid dry completely.
2. Color large sections of several meat trays with colorful markers; then snip the trays into small pieces.
3. Glue the Styrofoam pieces inside the box lid to make a colorful fall tree. Glue a few pieces along the bottom of the tree to look like scattered leaves.
4. Pin your finished project on a bulletin board.

"Whooo" Made These?

Make a fall bulletin board in a snap and recycle a little trash with the help of some fine feathered friends!

Steps:

1. Cut a 6" x 9" piece of red, yellow, orange, or brown construction paper.
2. Cut off the bottom corners of one short edge; then glue the cut pieces onto that edge to make feet.
3. Use craft glue to attach two bottle caps (or caps from liter bottles) to the paper to make eyes.
4. Cut off 1/3 of a plastic six-pack holder. Glue it around the owl's eyes (see illustration).
5. Use markers or crayons to draw feathers or other features on the owl.
6. Post your owl on a bulletin board that has been decorated with a large, cut-out tree.

Fall

Mask Masquerade

Your students won't be able to mask their joy when they've created these out-of-the-ordinary Halloween masks. For each student, cut eyes from an oval-shaped, thick paper plate. Using masking tape, attach a paint stirrer to each plate. Then layer strips of newsprint dipped in papier-mâché paste on the back of the plate to create facial features. When the features are formed as desired, top with strips of colored tissue paper which have been dipped in watered-down glue. For a dazzling sheen, spray the mask with varnish. Organize a Halloween parade so students can masquerade behind their original mask designs.

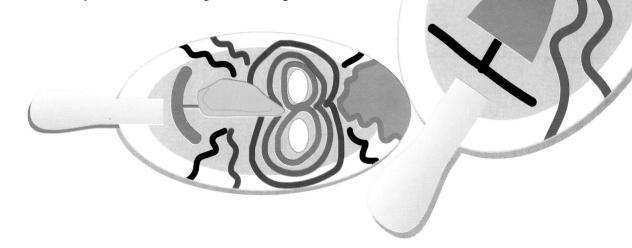

Stuffed Owls

If you give a hoot about having birds on your windowsill, you won't want to pass up this project! For each student, supply glue, yarn, a paper lunch bag, newspaper, one large construction-paper triangle, two small construction-paper triangles, and two construction-paper circles (or wiggle eyes). Have students stuff the bag with newspaper, tie it off at the bottom, and glue the pieces on as shown.

Leaf Prints

With this leaf printing suggestion, your youngsters can preserve fall's finery on fabric. Brush acrylic paint on several leaves. Then place the leaves, paint side up, on a newspaper-protected surface. Place an eight-inch square of white fabric atop the leaves and press without rubbing. Carefully lift the fabric and let it dry. Later add an original thought or verse using a fabric pen.

To frame this artwork, center a seven-inch tagboard square on a nine-inch square of felt. Trace the tagboard; then cut on the lines to create a felt frame. Glue the frame atop the white fabric and display.

Merrily, merrily, floating down
Leaves become paint spots on the ground.

Rub A Note

Although leaf rubbings are always popular this time of year, you can use this "old favorite" technique to create newfangled notecards. Fold a sheet of paper in half twice as shown. Flatten the paper out, and designate two of the resulting sections as the areas for rubbings. Place a leaf, vein side up, beneath the sheet of paper. Rub the paper with the side of an unwrapped crayon. Repeat this procedure, overlapping the rubbings and using different leaves and different colors. Refold the paper to create a notecard. You may want to keep a supply of students' notecards on hand to be used as thank-you notes or greeting cards, or just to add a special touch to any communication.

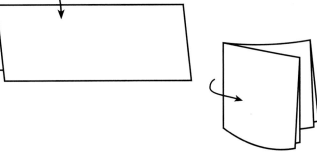

Fall

Gum Balls Galore

Those brown, prickly balls that fall from sweet gum trees can be converted into unique art projects. For a gum-ball spider, glue eight black, four-inch pipe cleaner sections into indentations. Add wiggle eyes to complete these creepy crawlers. Tie monofilament line to the gum ball's stem, and your spider can be suspended from bulletin-board tops, door moldings, or light fixtures.

Have your students exercise their creativity by using gum balls and miscellaneous craft supplies to create unique characters. There's no limit to the fun you can have with these critters.

Fall Foliage

Students can create a dramatic fall foliage display using construction paper and paint. Using the pattern on page 28, duplicate leaf patterns on yellow, orange, brown, and red construction paper. Cut out several leaves, crinkle them up, and soak them in water. Press each leaf flat on a protected desktop before dropping or painting irregular splotches of red, brown, orange, and yellow tempera paint on it. Crinkle the leaf in the palm of your hand again. Press each leaf flat on a protected surface and allow to dry. Display these leaves as embellishments or borders on classroom bulletin boards, or attach them to sheets of black construction paper for eye-catching displays.

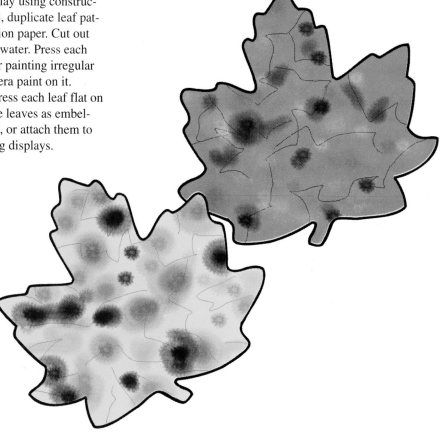

"Hoop-la!"

Do your classroom windows lack visual appeal? Add splashes of color at your windows to reflect a rainbow of seasonal moods. For each of these projects you'll need several embroidery hoops and cellophane, which is available in a variety of colors from art supply stores. (The use of "Easter basket" cellophane is not recommended. And acetate, which makes lovely projects, is too expensive for this purpose.)

To decorate your classroom windows for September, you'll need red cellophane (or tissue paper), monofilament line, cup hooks, embroidery hoops, glue, scissors, and green construction paper. In preparation for hanging your projects, attach cup hooks above each of your windows. To convert your supplies into gorgeous red apples, stretch red cellophane across each hoop, trim, and fasten snugly. Glue a green construction-paper leaf near the top of each hoop. Attach lengths of monofilament line to the tops of hoops, and make a loop in the top of each line for hanging. Suspend these eye-catching apples from the cup hooks for a razzle-dazzle display.

Each month thereafter, substitute different colors of cellophane or experiment with tissue paper, foils (for the holidays), doilies, waxed paper, and different construction-paper add-ons to give your classroom vastly different looks.

Fall

Look What I've Done!

Students will agree that these easy-to-make refrigerator magnets are perfect for displaying schoolwork. And what better way to receive positive recognition for their hard efforts! Using the patterns below, duplicate and cut out a pencil shape from tagboard and an eraser shape from pink construction paper. Glue the eraser cutout to the pencil cutout; then personalize and add details with markers. Attach a smiley sticker if desired. Laminate; then attach a piece of self-adhesive magnetic tape to the back of the cutout. There you have it—a personalized refrigerator magnet! Encourage students to show off several examples of work each week. To keep students actively interested in their refrigerator displays, make an apple magnet next month.

Patterns

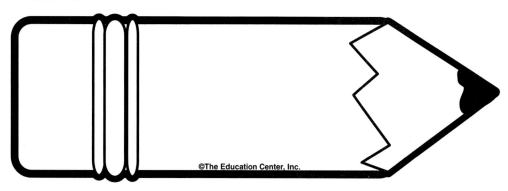

©The Education Center, Inc.

Duplicate the pencil pattern on colored tagboard.

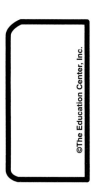

©The Education Center, Inc.

Trace an eraser pattern on pink construction paper.

©TEC

Trace a leaf pattern on green construction paper.

©TEC

Duplicate the apple pattern on red tagboard.

"Autumn-matic" Art

Add more dimension to your autumn art projects using paper plates as the background. Paint a thin paper plate blue using watercolor paint. Begin with a tan (or gold) construction-paper half-circle to match the diameter of the paper plate. Trim the half-circle; then glue to the rim of the paper plate to represent the foreground as shown. Next glue a brown, construction-paper tree cutout (pattern on page 28) to the foreground. Glue small bits of red, yellow, orange, and brown construction paper or tissue paper to the tree and foreground for leaves. Then attach a yellow circular cutout (sun) and white cotton balls (clouds) to the background. Add cutouts of people engaged in typical fall activities such as playing football, or add cutouts of typical fall sights such as baskets of apples or garden harvests. Staple yarn to the back of the paper plate for a hanger. These projects will "autumn-matically" be a hit with your students.

Centerpiece Show-Off

Perk up your room with student-made centerpieces just in time for Open House. Cut, or have students cut, construction-paper circles the same diameter as the doilies you'll use for this project. Glue each doily to a paper circle. (If doilies are not available, glue one construction-paper circle to another, smaller, paper circle of a contrasting color.) Glue bright, colorful leaves around the construction-paper circle. Top these creations with small student-decorated jack-o'-lanterns, gourds, or vases (plastic cups) of wildflowers. These cheery decorations are sure to set an upbeat atmosphere for your Open House guests.

Fall

"Apple-tizing" Artwork

Crunchy fall apples are the inspiration behind these bright masterpieces. Begin this project with red, yellow, and green tissue-paper squares. Cut several squares into apple shapes. Using liquid starch and a paintbrush, "paint" the tissue-paper apple cutouts onto white art paper. Overlap the cutouts as you cover the paper. The following day, brush on tempera-paint stems and leaves. Mount the completed projects atop slightly larger pieces of red construction paper. Now that's a feast for the eyes!

Marker Martians

When you're in the mood for an out-of-this-world art activity, give this one a try. Color one surface of a small, damp, sponge square with your favorite water-based marker. Press the sponge repeatedly onto the bottom of a luncheon-size paper plate. Reload the sponge with marker color whenever necessary. Use assorted sewing notions and arts-and-crafts items to decorate the plate bottom with facial features, hair, and antennae. When you're creating martians, the sky's the limit!

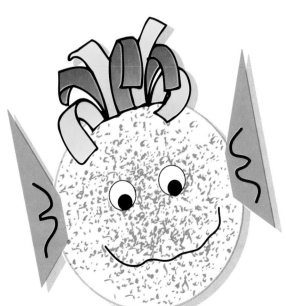

"Boo-tiful" Pencil Toppers

Delight your youngsters by having them create friendly spooks to give as gifts or to add a seasonal touch to their own pencils. Using the pattern on page 28, cut (or have students cut) two ghosts from white felt. With a fabric marker, add eyes and a mouth to one cutout. Then glue or stitch the two ghost cutouts together, leaving an opening at the bottom. When the glue is dry, slide the ghost atop a pencil. The little ghost just might motivate youngsters to do "boo-tiful" work!

Pumpkins From Paper

You don't have to have a green thumb to harvest a crop of prizewinning pumpkins—just a lot of paper. Wad up sheets of newspaper into a ball the size of a small pumpkin. Dip cut or torn newspaper strips into a flour-and-water mixture, and drape over the ball of newspaper. When dry, decorate with tempera paint. Add curling ribbon vines and green paper leaves. Wow! What a pumpkin patch!

fold

Black Cat Surprise

This Halloween kitty is "purrrrr-fectly" willing to sit up and pay attention in your October classroom. Trace the patterns (page 29) on black construction paper and cut out. Fold the larger pattern as shown. Glue on yellow construction paper or sequins for eyes, or attach wiggle-eyes. Glue six 1 1/2-inch pieces of thin spaghetti or pipe cleaners for the whiskers. When dry, lift the cat's head and glue only the top portion of the cat's legs to his body. Be sure to have the cat's legs extending just a little below his body. Set the kitty on a tabletop or windowsill among pumpkins or jack-o'-lanterns for an air of Halloween mystery.

Patterns

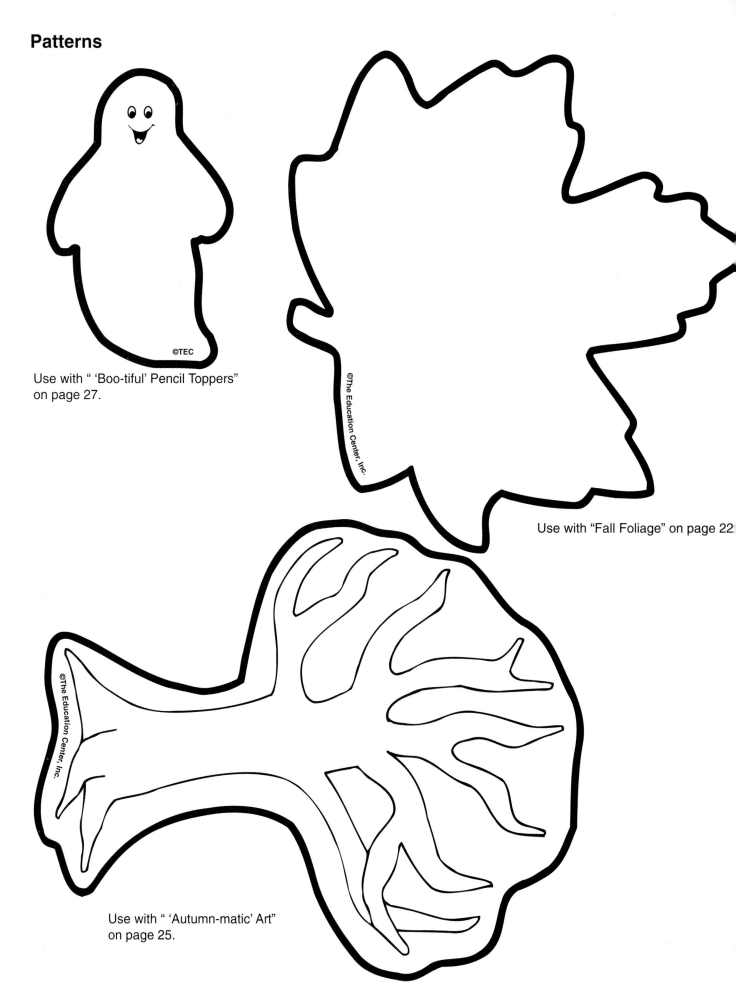

Use with " 'Boo-tiful' Pencil Toppers"
on page 27.

©TEC

©The Education Center, Inc.

Use with "Fall Foliage" on page 22

Use with " 'Autumn-matic' Art"
on page 25.

©The Education Center, Inc.

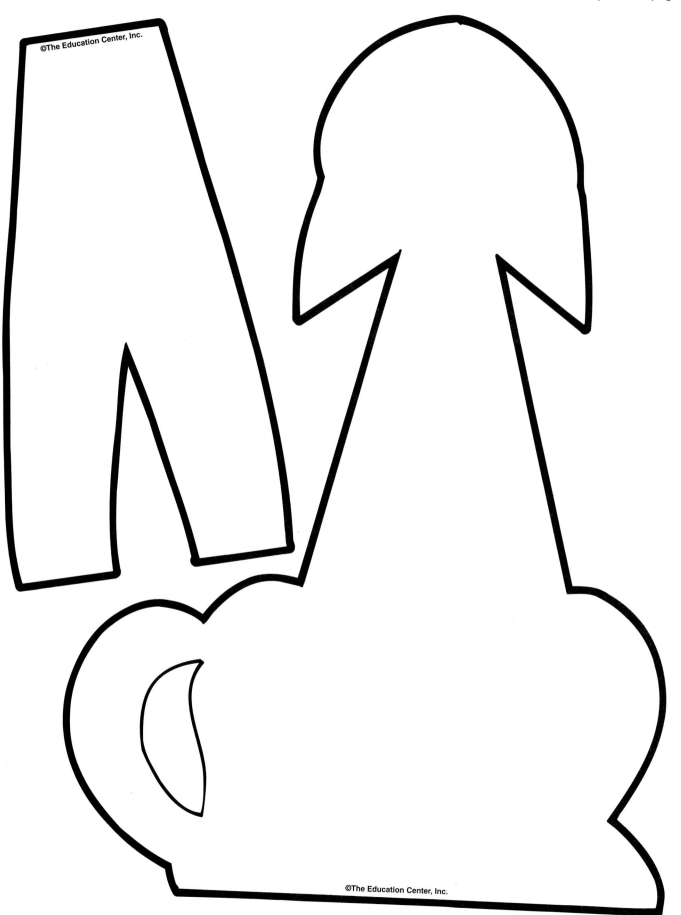

Fall

Personalized Pumpkins

Decorate your classroom with an unusual crop of signature pumpkins! Duplicate a pumpkin pattern on orange construction paper for your class; then have each student follow these steps.

Steps:
1. With a pencil, lightly write your name in the pumpkin shape. Use fat, bubble letters to completely fill in the pumpkin outline with your name.
2. Cut out your name, being careful not to cut through any letter.
3. Glue your name on a black piece of construction paper.
4. Add a green paper stem, vine, and leaves.

Ghosts In Flight

Create spooky scenes with cotton-ball ghosts. To begin, use colored chalk to draw a fall scene on black construction paper. Take the artwork outdoors and spray it with fixative or hairspray. When the paper is dry, gently pull to stretch a cotton ball into a ghostlike shape. Glue the cotton to the fall scene. For eyes, glue tiny black circles made with a hole puncher onto the cotton. Add other ghosts in a similar manner for a haunting effect.

Torn Up About Jack-O'-Lanterns

Here's a Halloween art idea your youngsters will love to get torn up about. Play some Halloween music or a story tape as you have youngsters tear orange tissue paper into approximately nickel-size pieces. You will also need both yellow and green tissue paper pieces. To create this haunting masterpiece, draw a circle on black construction paper and spread glue to fill the circle. Press enough orange paper pieces on the glue to cover; then glue the yellow paper atop the orange paper to create the jack-o'-lantern's face. Add a green paper stem in the same manner. How's that for haunting results?

Spiders

Here are some creepy-crawlies that will add an eerie effect to your October classroom. To prepare craft sticks for spider legs, cut them in half and spray them with black paint. To make dough for spiders, mix two cups of flour, one cup of salt, black tempera paint, and just enough water to create a doughlike consistency. To assemble a spider, mold some dough into the shape of a spider body; then insert the cut ends of eight craft stick pieces into the dough. Eyes and additional details may be painted on when the dough is sufficiently hardened.

Fall

Eerie Nights!

Create eerie night scenes with this simple, fun technique. Give each child a 5" x 8" sheet of white paper and a straw. Have students place a few blobs of black paint on their papers. Students then blow briskly through their straws, spreading the paint into spooky, jagged formations. Have each child trace, cut, and paste a shining, yellow moon and the silhouette of a soaring black bat on his paper. Mount pictures on 6" x 9" black backgrounds.

Triangle Tricks

Challenge students to create designs made up entirely of triangles. Each student will need a 9" x 12" sheet of black construction paper for the background and orange and yellow paper for the triangle cutouts. Instruct students to cut and paste triangles so that more triangles are formed by the open spaces of black background. This project requires planning and thinking as students work, but they'll be proud of their final products!

Jolly, Jazzy Jacks

These jazzy jack-o'-lanterns will brighten up any classroom! Use oil pastels to create a colorful design of wide and narrow lines on white paper. Cover with a thin wash of pale green paint. When dry, cut into a pumpkin shape. Use scraps of yellow and orange construction paper to cut and paste jack-o'-lantern features. Mount on an orange background and add a brown paper stem.

Black Cat Bookmarks

Create these fun bookmarks, perfect for the holiday season or anytime. Reproduce the cat pattern for each child. Then have students follow the steps below to complete their bookmarks.

Steps:

1. Trace the cat pattern onto black construction paper and cut out.
2. Use a hole puncher to make eyes and a mouth.
3. Use a pencil point to make two sets of holes for the whiskers.
4. To make the whiskers, pull two 2-inch-long pieces of white yarn through the holes.
5. Glue the black cat to sturdy orange paper; glue only from the head down to the middle of the body.
6. Add black dots for the pupils of the eyes.
7. Cut around the cat, leaving about a 1/4-inch margin of orange paper around the cat's body and a 3/4-inch margin around the tail.
8. Slip the tail over the page that you want to mark in a book.

Pattern

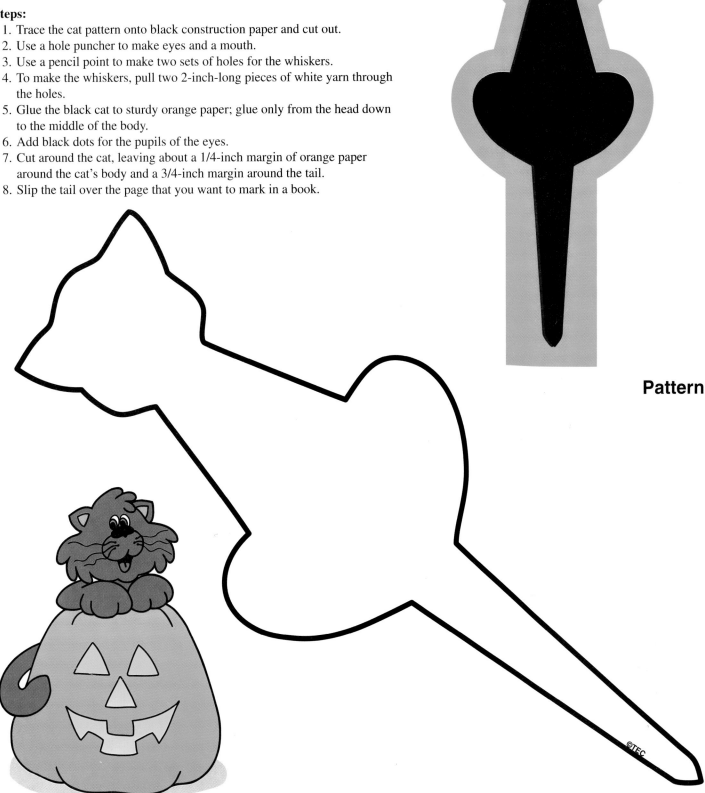

Fall

Creepy Crawlies

Not one youngster will try to wriggle away from this art project. To make a creepy crawly, begin by tearing tissue paper into strips. Using thinned glue and a paintbrush, glue the strips on a 4" x 18" piece of white construction paper. Occasionally overlap the tissue-paper strips. Once each strip is attached to the paper, brush a layer of glue atop it. The following day, fold the paper in half and trim to round the ends. Decorate one rounded end with pipe-cleaner antennae, a tissue-paper topknot, and facial features made from assorted art supplies. Accordion-fold the paper. Whether you use your creepy crawlies to brighten up classroom windowsills, bookcases, tabletops, or bulletin boards, they're certain to be lively conversation pieces!

fold

Leafy Lanterns

Suspend these lanterns for a spectacular array of fall foliage. Place bright, colorful leaves atop the waxy surface of a 9" x 12" sheet of waxed paper. Cover the leaves with a second sheet of waxed paper, turning the waxy surface to the inside. Using a press cloth, carefully iron (at a low setting) the outer surface of the waxed paper until the leaves are held in place by melted wax. Fold in half two 2" x 12" strips of yellow, red, orange, or brown construction paper. Insert the upper and lower edges of the waxed paper into the folds of the construction-paper strips and glue in place. Form a cylinder by overlapping and stapling together the ends of each construction-paper strip. For an eye-catching display, attach a 1" x 8" construction-paper handle to the top of the lantern as shown. Attach a length of monofilament line to each lantern handle and suspend from paper clips or cup hooks attached to the ceiling.

Adapt this idea to create lanterns that "glow" with seasonal paper cutouts such as snowflakes, hearts, or shamrocks.

Give A Hoot!

Attract parents to Open House festivities or parent conferences with these adorable, student-made owl magnets. Flatten a small portion of baking dough (see recipe below) to approximately 1/2-inch thickness. Cut a circle about 2 1/4 inches in diameter from the dough for the owl face. (Use the pattern below or press an inverted plastic glass of a similar size into the dough.) Pull away excess dough; then use your thumb and index finger to pinch two eye sockets into the center of the circle. Brush lightly with egg (to achieve a golden color while baking) and bake in a 300° oven until hardened (approximately one hour). When cool, use tempera paint to create an orange triangular beak and white eye sockets. When dry, securely fasten a wiggle eye in each socket.

Duplicate the remaining owl patterns onto tagboard, cut out, and use as tracers to transfer each pattern onto appropriate colors of tagboard. Assemble the owl body as shown. Use a hot glue gun to affix the face and a magnetic strip to the owl body. Personalize the owl as desired. Display the owl magnets during Open House or parent conferences along with a note to each parent from his child. Have parents place the magnets on their home refrigerators to display their children's work.

Baking Dough Recipe

2 cups flour
1 cup salt
1 cup cold water

Mix enough water with the dry ingredients to make a dough.

Patterns

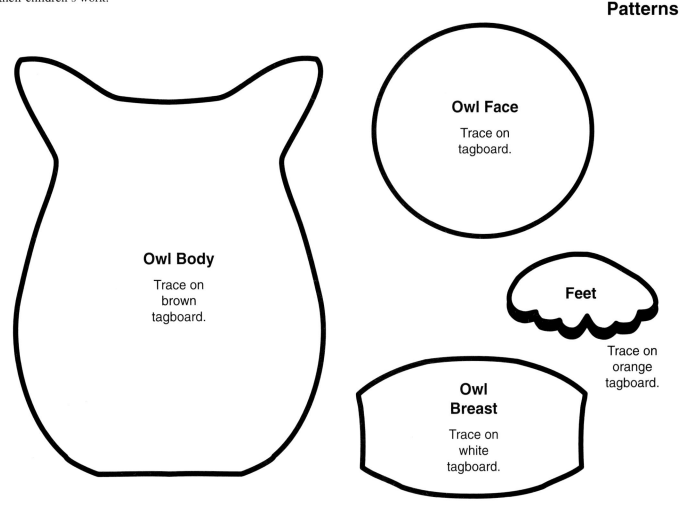

Owl Body

Trace on brown tagboard.

Owl Face

Trace on tagboard.

Feet

Trace on orange tagboard.

Owl Breast

Trace on white tagboard.

Cornfield Guard

As the corn tassels turn to golden brown, turn your youngsters' harvest thoughts to bushels of creative fun. Have each student make a scarecrow using the directions below. If desired, youngsters may also mount colored crow cutouts (pattern on page 37) atop their scarecrows. Caw! Caw!

To make the scarecrow's overalls:
1. Make an overalls template using the pattern on page 37.
2. Place the template on a folded 9" x 12" sheet of blue construction paper as directed on the pattern.
3. Trace and cut on the resulting outline.

To make the scarecrow's arms:
1. Fold a 12" x 2 1/4" strip of red construction paper in half (to 6" x 2 1/4").
2. Cut two notches near the unfolded end as shown.

To make the scarecrow's face and hat:
1. Cut out and decorate a tan circle approximately 5 1/2" in diameter.
2. Place the hat template on a folded 7" square of yellow construction paper as directed on the pattern on page 37.
3. Trace and cut on the resulting outline.

To assemble and complete the scarecrow:
1. Glue the scarecrow's red paper arms to the back of the overalls, the face to the top of the overalls, and the hat to the top of the head.
2. Glue 2 1/2" x 1/2" yellow paper strips to the backs of the pant bottoms, sleeves, and face.
3. Glue small paper squares atop the overalls and the shirt. Add stitches with crayon.

Hoot Owls

Here's an art project that won't ruffle any feathers! To make an owl, fold and glue three corners of a 9" brown paper square so that they touch in the center of the paper. For tail feathers, use scissors to fringe the unfolded corner. Gently pull some of the fringes forward and some backward for dimension. For the owl's beak, fold a 1 1/2" orange paper square in half diagonally and glue it on. For eyes, cut two 2 1/2" yellow paper circles and two 2 3/4" black paper circles. Glue each yellow circle atop a black one. Use a black marker to make a pea-size dot in the center of each yellow circle before gluing each eye in place. Create a spooky spectacle by displaying your youngsters' owls perched on a bare tree cutout.

Use with "Cornfield Guard" on page 36.

©TEC
Place dotted line on fold. Do not cut.
overalls
©The Education Center, Inc.
Place dotted line on fold. Do not cut.
hat
©The Education Center, Inc.

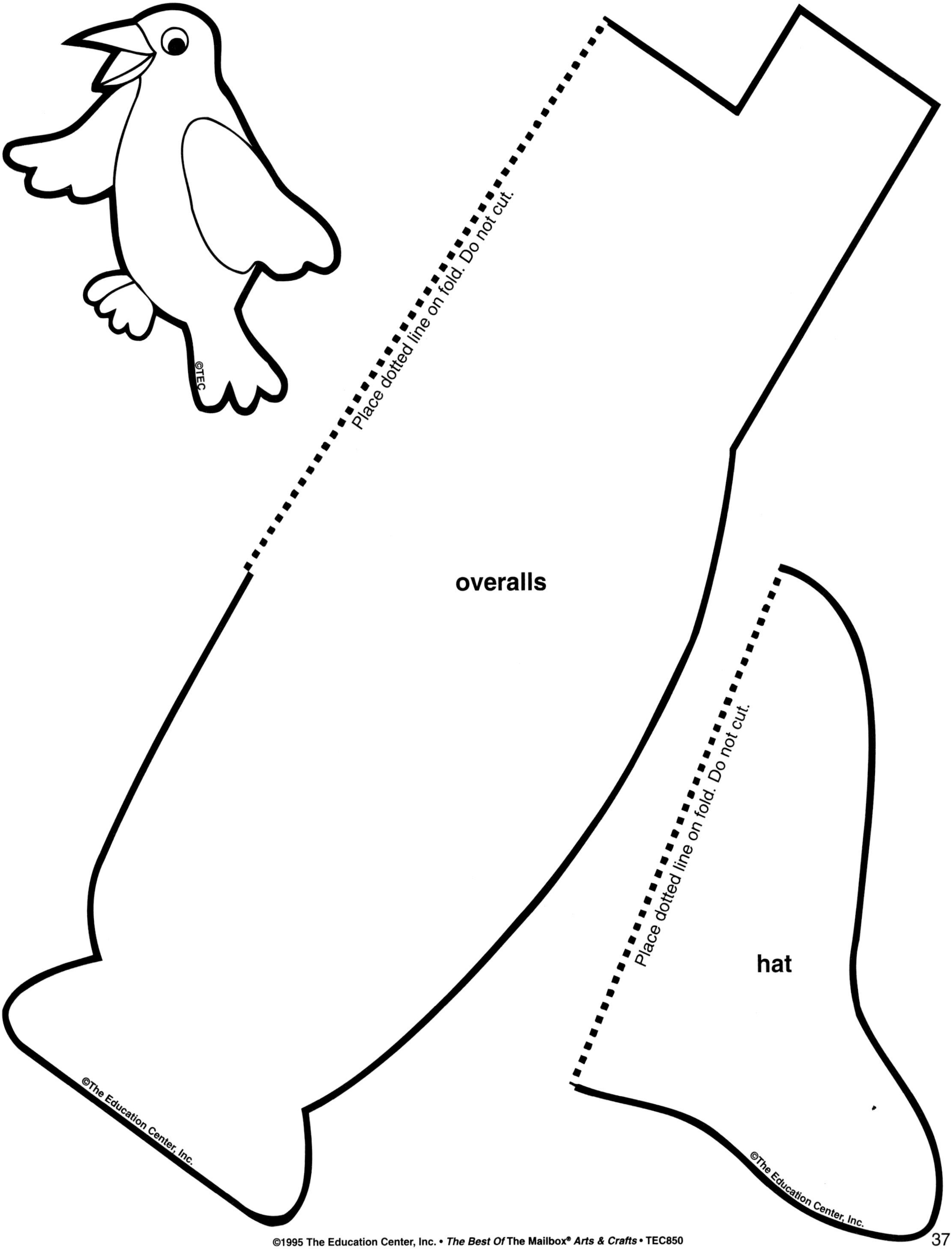

Fall

Spooky Carbon Crayon Resist

Here's a fun art project that requires used duplicating carbons. Distribute used carbons and white sheets of paper to students. Have each student place the white paper atop the carbon (carbon side up) and draw a Halloween design. Throw out the carbons and turn the papers over. Have students color their designs with crayons. When finished, have students hold their artwork under running water. The carbon will wash over the picture, creating a resist effect. (Be sure to have rubber gloves available to keep ink off hands!) Let drawings dry; then display them in your classroom.

Sculptured Jack-O'-Lanterns

Your students will enjoy making these three-dimensional, paper-sculpture jack-o'-lanterns! Give each student eight one-inch strips of orange construction paper. Staple the strips together at the tops. Have students curl, glue, and staple strips to make the outline and features of the jack-o'-lantern. Attach string and hang the pumpkins from the ceiling, or pin them to a bulletin board.

Illuminating Art

This cut-out window art project is sure to lure everyone's attention!

Materials: dark bulletin-board paper (enough to cover your classroom window), art knives, orange tissue paper, tape, flat board for cutting surface

Steps:
1. Place the board under the bulletin-board paper.
2. Have students cut Halloween designs (scary faces, etc.) into the paper with art knives.
3. When designs are completed, tape the tissue paper behind them.
4. Tape the paper to a window, and enjoy the frightfully fun display!

Witch Heads

Create fun desk ornaments for the Halloween season!

Materials: one balloon per student, green tissue-paper squares and strips, glue, construction paper (for eyes), margarine container, black construction paper, scissors, pencil, water

Steps:
1. Thin glue with water.
2. Blow up balloon and tie off.
3. Dip squares of green tissue paper into glue and attach to balloon until completely covered.
4. Mold nose with strips of green tissue paper and glue.
5. Attach construction-paper eyes.
6. Cut large cone shape from black construction paper and staple to make hat.
7. Attach hat to balloon head.
8. Curl black construction-paper strips with pencil and glue to balloon for hair.
9. Set in open margarine container to dry.

Fall

Sleepy Hollow Forest

Create an eerie sensation with this artwork reminiscent of the dark and twisted trees in Sleepy Hollow, where poor ol' Ichabod Crane met his tragic fate. On art paper, drip some thinned, black tempera paint or black watercolor paint. Blow through a drinking straw to transform the paint drips into the shapes of gnarly trees. While this dries, cut out and decorate several orange construction-paper jack-o'-lanterns. Complete the ghastly effect by gluing jack-o'-lanterns to the tree artwork.

If you're a little more adventurous, heighten the eerie effect by having students create the tree branches atop painted backgrounds. To prepare a spooky-looking background sky, use a wide brush to paint the upper two-thirds of a sheet of art paper purple. Then paint the lower one-third pink, blending it into the purple, and brush a few pink streaks atop the purple. When dry, this uncanny October sky is ready for trees.

Airborne Witches

Get your Halloween party off the ground with airborne witches. To make a paper "airplane," fold a 9" x 12" sheet of black construction paper as shown. Decorate a two-inch green construction-paper circle with a witch's facial features. Then glue several lengths of heavy, black, gift-wrapping yarn to the circle for hair. Before gluing the circle to the paper airplane, glue a 1/2" x 3" strip of black paper atop the yarn as shown. Have each student label his witch.

For a delightful party game, mark *start* and *finish* lines on the floor and line up your youngsters with their witches. Have students say the chant (right), releasing their witches on the last line. It's great Halloween frivolity!

There's a funny old lady
  with a pointed hat.
At my door she went rap,
  rap, rap.
I was going to the door to
  see who was there,
When off on her broom-
  stick she flew through
  the air.

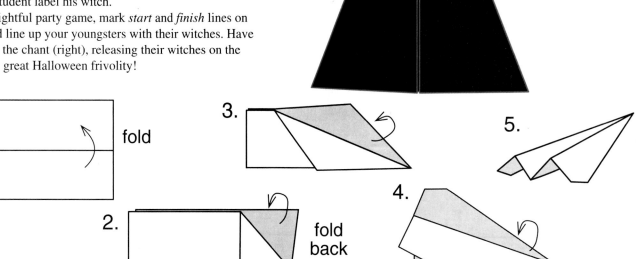

1. fold

2.

3.

fold
back

4.

5.

Bat Mobiles

Your classroom will have more bats than a belfry when these mobiles are flitting to and fro in schoolroom breezes. Without changing the shape of the hook or the bottom part, gently bend both sides of a coat hanger downward. Place the hanger near the upper edge of a half-sheet of black tissue paper. Squeeze a thin trail of glue around the hanger; then fold up the lower half of the tissue-paper sheet to cover the hanger. Press lightly so the glue will grip the paper all the way around the hanger. The following day, trim the excess paper from the hanger. For wings, glue a few tissue-paper strips on each side of the hanger. Complete the mobile by gluing on additional paper features.

To vary this idea, bend a coat hanger into a ghostlike shape. Using a whole sheet of white tissue paper, complete the ghost similarly to the bat.

"Ghostly" Wind Sock

Want to create an eerie spectacle in your October classroom? These ghostly wind socks may be just what you're looking for. To make a hanger for a wind sock, poke a hole in the bottom center of a white paper bag. Tie one end of a yarn length to a paper clip; then insert the other end into the hole from inside the bag. Pull the yarn to the outside of the bag, and loop and knot it. Position the bag so that the hanger is at the top. Flatten the bag; then glue on paper facial features and scallop the bag's opening. Glue eight 12" x 3/4" tissue-paper strips to the inside of the scalloped opening. Hang these wind socks from the ceiling for all to enjoy the specter of poltergeists as they eerily bob and billow in the autumn breeze.

Fall

Jack-O'-Lantern Delights

Here's a great idea to have in your Halloween bag of tricks. Use pinking shears to cut three inches from the top of an orange, lunch-size, paper bag. (If necessary, substitute a white paper bag which has been painted or colored orange.) On one side of the bag, sketch and cut out jack-o'-lantern facial-feature outlines. To the top, staple a green construction-paper stem and curling ribbon "vines." Line the bag with yellow tissue paper. Scatter student-made jack-o'-lanterns throughout your classroom for a delectable display. On Halloween day, deposit a few treats (candies, stickers, pencils, etc.) into each student's jack-o'-lantern. In little more time than it takes to say, "Bibbity, bobbity, boo!", orange paper bags have become jack-o'-lantern delights.

Paper-Strip Jack-O'-Lantern

Create jack-o'-lanterns a bit differently this year! To begin, arrange eight orange paper strips (9" x 1/4") as shown on a sheet of black construction paper. Then cut facial features and a stem from scrap paper. Glue the cutouts in place to finish the project. Why are you grinning, Mr. Jack-O'-Lantern?

Bewitching Beauties

Dangle these projects from your classroom ceiling to create a bewitchingly whimsical effect. Depending upon the ability levels of your children, you may want to have students make only one part of the witch at a time and assemble the parts on another day.

To make the body:
1. Fold a 12" x 18" sheet of black construction paper in half lengthwise.
2. Beginning at the fold, cut parallel slits approximately 1 1/2" apart.
3. Unfold the paper, overlap the ends to create a tubular shape, and staple in place.

To make the head:
1. Fold a 4 1/2" x 12" sheet of green construction paper in half along its width.
2. Trim to round each corner of the folded piece. (The folded area will be the top of the witch's head.)
3. Glue on marker-embellished construction-paper facial features and tissue-paper hair.

To make the hat:
1. Fold a 4 1/2" x 12" sheet of black construction paper in half along its width.
2. Draw a hat shape on the paper as shown. Cut on the outline, leaving part of the folded area uncut.
3. Attach Halloween stickers to decorate the hat.

To assemble and display:
1. Glue the hat-shaped halves together, sandwiching the upper part of the witch's head in the hat brim.
2. Glue the witch's head to the body.
3. Embellish the witch, if desired, with hand, broom, and/or magic wand cutouts.
4. Punch a hole near the top of the hat, and suspend the witch from the ceiling.

Bare Bones

Make no bones about it! Drawing a skeleton isn't nearly as hard as it's cracked up to be. Set the stage for this activity by reading *Funnybones* by Janet and Allan Ahlberg. Then have students complete this project one step at a time, as you demonstrate. To make a skeleton, accordion-fold a 6" x 18" strip of black construction paper so that the paper is visually divided into eight (approximately 2 1/4") strips. Unfold a portion of the paper as shown. Using a white crayon, draw the upper skull onto the unfolded section, referring to the sample diagram. Unfold the second section of paper, conceal the third section, and draw the lower half of the skull, referring to the diagram. Continue drawing one section at a time until the entire skeleton is complete. Chances are, you'll be surprised by how well these skeleton drawings turn out.

Turkey Cutups

Gobblers of a different feather result from this fold-and-cut method. Each child will need an 18" x 24" sheet of construction paper, folded in half (18-inch sides touching), and a pair of scissors. To help students get started, sketch an outline on the board as shown. Students then use light-colored pencils to draw various other outlines and shapes, keeping in mind that the halves of the turkeys are symmetrical. With the paper still folded, cut along the lines to remove all outlined parts, making inside cuts first. Finish the turkey by cutting on the outermost lines. Use a hole puncher to make the eyes. Unfold and mount on a contrasting color for display.

On A Roll

Create a unique mosaic gobbler with rolled-paper "tiles." To make the rolls, cut a supply of one-half-inch-wide construction-paper strips of different colors, 15 or 16 inches long. Coil tightly and glue the ends to hold. Glue to a colored background of lightweight cardboard or poster board.

Yarn Masks

Uncommon masks result from using a few common materials. Use a sturdy paper plate for the base of this symmetrically designed mask. Draw and cut out outlines for the eyes, nose, and mouth. Staple yarn ties to the sides of the plate; then glue various colors of yarn strips to the front. Display finished projects on a "Who's Behind That Mask?" bulletin board.

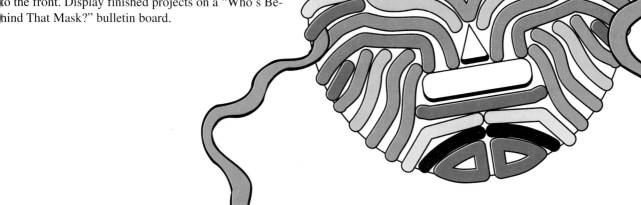

What A Gorgeous Gobbler!

Use a tried-and-true art technique to create a gallery of gorgeous gobblers! Have each student completely color a large piece of white paper with brightly colored crayons, bearing down hard while coloring. Next have the student coat his entire paper with black crayon, also bearing down hard. Have the child use a knitting needle or pointed wooden skewer to scratch a turkey design on his paper. Encourage students to scratch lots of detail in the feathers. Mount the finished gobblers on bright colors of paper.

Fowls From Filters

Making these gobblers is not only an artistic endeavor—it's also an exercise in listening and following directions. Referring to the materials list, provide the necessary supplies. Read aloud and demonstrate each step of the oral directions. For display, these turkeys may be glued or stapled to sheets of construction paper.

Materials needed for each turkey:

coffee filter
5" brown construction-paper square   water
3" brown construction-paper square   scissors
2" yellow construction-paper square   glue
3" x 1" red construction-paper rectangle   marker
watercolor paint set with brush

Oral Instructions:

1. Paint a line from the center of the filter to the outer edge. Change colors and do this over and over. It's okay for the colors to run into each other. Set the filter aside to dry. This will be the turkey's feathers.
2. Trim off the corners of each brown square to make a circle.
3. For the turkey's body, glue the larger brown circle to the bottom of the filter.
4. For the turkey's head, glue the smaller brown circle to the filter. The smaller circle should overlap the larger one just a little.
5. For legs, cut two thin strips from the edge of the yellow square. Set the legs aside.
6. Fold the remaining yellow rectangle in half. Draw a giant capital *v* on the paper as shown. Cut on the *v*. The folded piece is the turkey's beak. Two of the triangles are feet. You will not need the other two.
7. Glue each triangle foot to a leg.
8. Glue the legs to the turkey's body. Then glue the beak to the turkey's head.
9. Cut a wiggly-shaped wattle from the red rectangle. Glue it by the beak.
10. Use a marker to draw the turkey's eyes.

Steps 1, 2, 3, and 4.

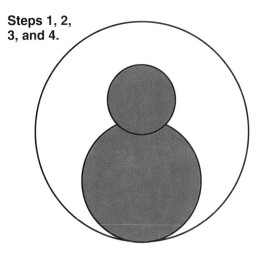

Step 5.

legs

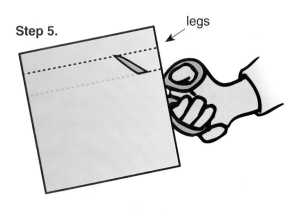

Step 6.

beak

feet

feet

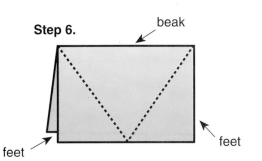

Nature Turkeys

To feather these turkeys, take your students on a nature hike around the school. Instruct students to gather a supply of different leaves. Back in the classroom, provide students with sturdy art paper and glue. Each student glues leaves onto his paper in the shape of a turkey's feathers. He then adds the head, body, and legs to complete the project. Display these grandiose gobblers on a bulletin board entitled "Birds Of A Different Feather."

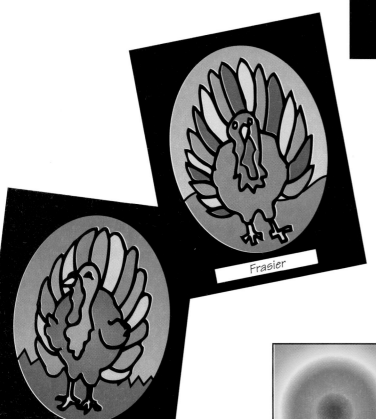

Frasier

Ellen

Oval Frames

Turn your students' artwork into a professional-looking display. Cut ovals in 12" x 18" sheets of black construction paper. Place the frames over student artwork on bulletin boards or walls. Add nametags to finish the display. Your students will marvel at this elegant touch!

Gobble Gobble Gallery

Just in time for Thanksgiving, have your youngsters create an entire flock of grinning gobblers from scratch. To make a scratchboard turkey, begin with a 5" x 7" poster-board rectangle. Using red, orange, yellow, green, purple, and blue crayons, heavily color a bull's-eye pattern to cover your poster board. Atop this, apply a thick coat of black crayon. Reapply black crayon, if necessary, to cover the brighter colors. Cut a toothpick in half. Alternately use the resulting "thick" and "thin" toothpick ends to "scratch" a turkey design on the crayon-covered board. Mount the completed turkey scratchboards onto contrasting tagboard for display. Great gobblers! Look what you've scratched up!

Fall

Turkey Tees

Whether youngsters create these turkey T-shirts as a follow-up to a farm field trip or a story about Thanksgiving turkeys, they'll undoubtedly be a gobblin' triumph. To make a handprint turkey, paint the palm side of a hand using brown acrylic paint or fabric paint. Press the hand, with fingers spread, onto a T-shirt that has been washed and dried. When the paint on the shirt has dried, use fabric markers to add eyes, a wattle, feet, and colorful feathers. Set the design with a warm iron.

Your youngsters will delight in having one of these shirts to take home. But consider extending the fun by having each child make and decorate an additional handprint on a shirt in your size. (Your paraprofessional will need one too!) The day before Thanksgiving you'll know exactly what to wear!

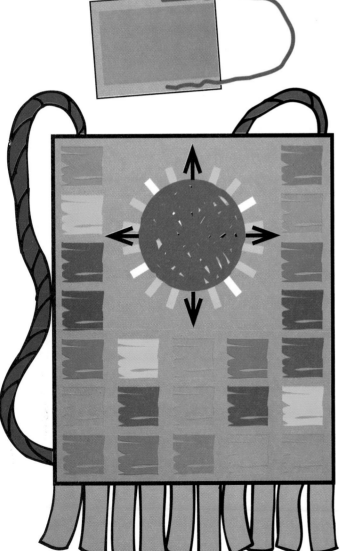

Pouches From The Past

Have students create these pouches reminiscent of the ones Native Americans used about the time of the first Thanksgiving. To prepare for this activity, cut the front and back panels from large, brown, paper grocery bags into 6" x 7" and 6" x 10" pieces For each pouch you will also need a 36" length of brown yarn or cord.

To assemble a pouch, glue a 6" x 7" bag piece around three sides, leaving a short side without glue. Place the yarn ends atop the glue as shown; then place a 6" x 10" bag piece atop the smaller one so that the extra length extends below the smaller piece. When the glue is dry, snip the extra length for fringe. For decoration, use crayon to draw on the sides of the pouch. Iron each pouch between sheets of newsprint to complete the effect.

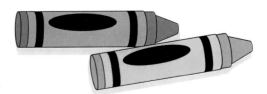

Turkey Sun Catchers

You'll hear lots of ooohs and aaahs from your students as they create these grand gobblers. To make a turkey's tail feathers, begin by coloring a coffee filter with watercolor markers. Fold the filter in half four times. Immerse the point of the folded filter into a bowl of water and watch as the water seeps upward, bleeding the colors. Unfold the filter and set it aside to dry. Cut a turkey body from a brown construction-paper copy of the pattern below. Glue it to the dried filter along with feet, a beak, eyes, and a wattle cut from construction paper. Personalize the turkey if desired.

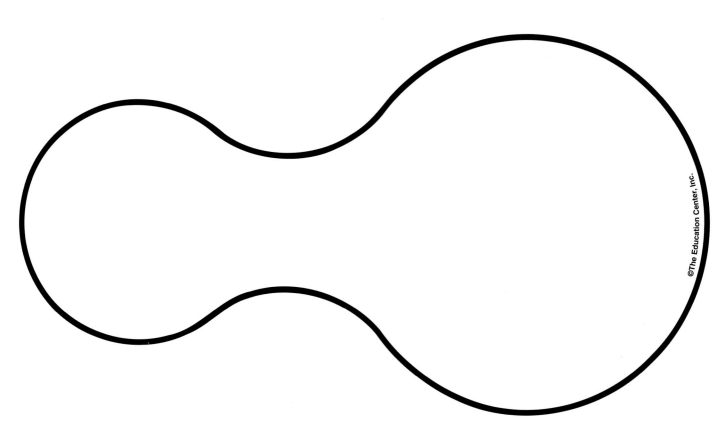

©The Education Center, Inc.

Fall

Three-Dimensional Turkeys

Scratchin' around for turkey art projects for your student gobblers to try? Then look no further. To make a three-dimensional turkey, first cut a half-circle from a sheet of 9" x 12" brown construction paper; then curl it into a cone shape and staple. Glue a wooden ice-cream spoon to the cone for the turkey's head. Attach wiggle eyes and a folded, yellow diamond-shaped beak to the spoon. Then cut six 6" x 2" rectangles into feather shapes and staple them to the back of the cone. To complete the turkey, glue two yellow, folded, diamond-shaped feet to the front bottom portion of the cone. It's turkey time!

Bill Of Rights Wind Sock

Celebrate Bill Of Rights Day on December 15 with a fun wind sock project.

Materials:

five 15" x 1 1/2" red tissue-paper strips	glue
five 15" x 1 1/2" white tissue-paper strips	string for hanging
one 6" x 18" blue construction-paper strip	self-sticking stars (optional)
one 4" x 18" white construction-paper strip	hole puncher
	fine-tipped marker

Steps:

1. Write an amendment on each tissue-paper strip.
2. Write "Bill Of Rights" in large letters across the white construction-paper strip.
3. Glue the white strip onto the blue strip.
4. Turn the blue strip over. Arrange the red and white tissue-paper strips alternately at the bottom of the blue section.
5. Glue the tissue strips in place.
6. Glue the ends of the blue section together to form a cylinder.
7. Decorate the cylinder with self-sticking stars if desired.
8. Punch holes in opposite sides of the cylinder and add string; then hang the wind sock from the ceiling or a bulletin board for others to enjoy.

Wonderful Wallpaper Wreaths

For a holiday project, have each student fold a wallpaper sample; then have him cut holly-shaped leaves from the folded sample. The student glues the leaves in a layered pattern onto a cardboard circle. (Cut the centers from the circles with an art knife before beginning the project.) After the glue is completely dry, have students spray glitter on the wreaths and add paper bows.

Sparkling Menorahs

Add sparkle to your classroom with this unique Hanukkah project!

Materials for each student:

copy of the pattern on page 52
clear plastic wrap
12-inch-wide strip of aluminum foil
permanent markers
8 1/2" x 10" piece of tagboard
tape

Steps:

1. Center the menorah pattern on the tagboard. Tape it securely.
2. Place plastic wrap tightly over the pattern. Wrap it around to the back of the tagboard and tape it securely in place.
3. Color the menorah with permanent markers. Fill in the picture first; then outline each part of the menorah with a black marker to prevent smearing.
4. Gently remove the plastic wrap and pattern from the tagboard and set them aside.
5. Lightly crumple the piece of foil. Smooth out the foil and use it to cover the tagboard. Secure the foil to the back of the tagboard with tape.
6. Re-cover the tagboard with the plastic wrap, taping it securely on the back. Make sure the plastic wrap is pulled as tight as possible.

Pattern

Use with "Sparkling Menorahs" on page 51.

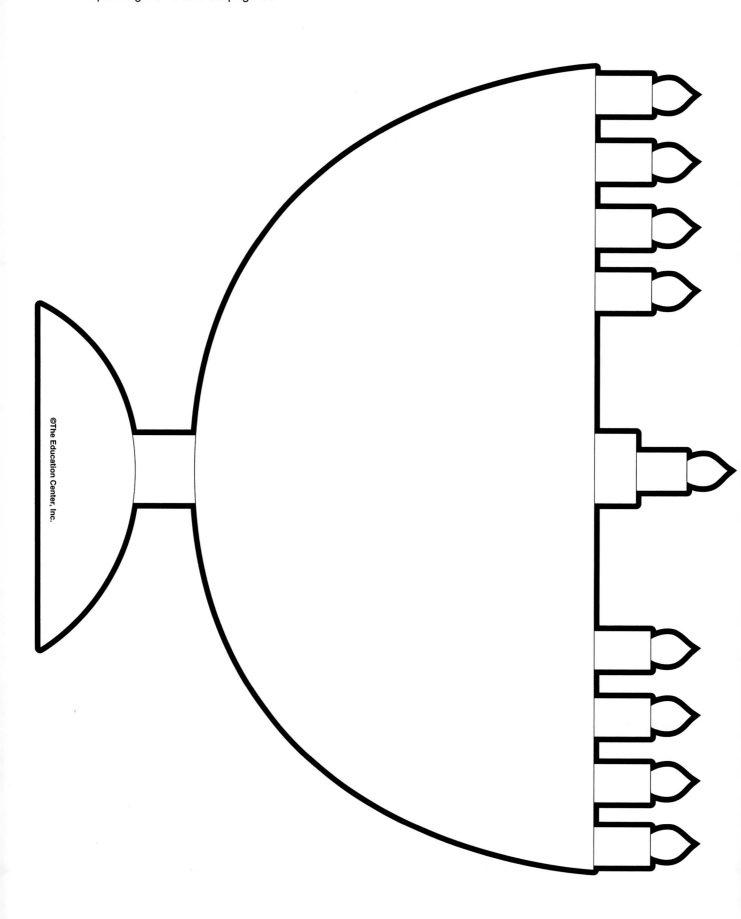

©The Education Center, Inc.

Ho! Ho! Ho!

Gee, Santa! Is your nose frostbitten? To make a Santa, use an X-acto® knife to cut a small *x* in the center of a paper plate bottom. Dip cotton balls into glue; then press them onto the plate bottom. Repeat this process until half of the plate bottom is covered with cotton balls. Allow the glue to dry. Poke an uninflated red balloon through the previously cut *x*. Inflate the balloon, tie it, and tape it in place. Draw on eyes or attach wiggle eyes. Cut out a red construction-paper hat. Trim it with cotton balls; then attach the hat above Santa's eyes. It must be Saint Nick!

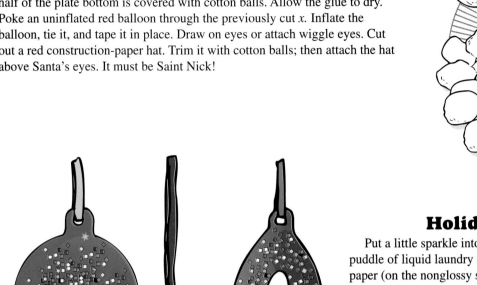

Holiday Finger Paint

Put a little sparkle into your holiday finger-paint projects. Pour a puddle of liquid laundry starch in the middle of a sheet of butcher paper (on the nonglossy side). Have your students spread the starch by hand. Then have students sprinkle dry tempera paint out of shaker bottles with large holes (such as minced onion bottles) onto the starch, and blend. Sprinkle glitter onto the wet paint. When dry, cut the finger-painted paper into ornament shapes and display. Now that's eye-catching art!

Personalized Wreath Banners

Here's a holiday decoration your youngsters can really get into! Protect a large area of the classroom floor with newspapers. Into a dishpan, pour a thin layer of a green tempera and liquid soap mixture. Place a 2 1/2' length of white bulletin-board paper on the protected floor and draw an 18"-diameter circle in the center. Have a youngster step barefooted into the dishpan. Then have him walk around the circle, taking tiny steps. He may need to go around the circle more than once to create a full-looking "wreath." Allow the green paint to dry. The following day, pour a thin layer of red paint and liquid soap mixture into a dishpan. Have the child press his hands into the paint, and then repeatedly press his hands onto the paper to create a bow shape. Also have him randomly put red thumbprints on the wreath for berries. When the wreath is dry, have the child write his name using a red marker or a glitter pen. To complete the banner, have the youngster repeatedly snip the lower edge for a frayed effect; then glue a wooden dowel to the top, attach yarn, and hang.

Winter ❄ ❄

Peppermint Reindeer

This reindeer may be made of paper, but you can practically smell the peppermint. Trace a candy cane shape onto a 12" x 18" sheet of white construction paper. Cut out the shape; then use a crayon or a marker to add stripes. For the reindeer's antlers, trace the shapes of your hands onto brown construction paper, and cut on the outlines. Glue the hand cutouts to the back of the cane cutout. For a nose, glue on a glittered construction-paper circle or a pom-pom. Add an eye to complete the reindeer.

Wreaths With Personality

For this project, ask each child to bring a large brown bag, three yards of one-inch-wide fabric ribbon, and three more yards of 1 1/2-inch-wide ribbon (optional). Provide holiday-related decorations. To begin, cut a grocery bag down one side and cut to detach the bottom. Flatten the remaining paper; then roll it from a longer side. To form a wreath, bring the ends of the roll together and staple them in place. Wrap one-inch ribbon around the paper wreath and secure the ends. Use the remaining ribbon to create a bow if desired. Attach the bow and the decorations to the wreath. (If desired, speed this process along by using a hot glue gun. Be certain to caution your youngsters about the hazards associated with this process.) Bend and twist a pipe cleaner at the top of the wreath for hanging.

Santa Napkin Holders

How proud each of your youngsters will be as he takes home these festive napkin holders that he fashioned himself! To prepare for this activity, duplicate the patterns on page 55 as directed. To make a napkin holder, cut and fold a copy of the cap as indicated. Then cut out and glue the remaining pieces and some hole-punched holly berries as shown. (Cutting with pinking shears will add a unique appearance to the pom-pom, greenery, and fur trimming.) Tuck a napkin inside the folded cap so that the napkin flares outward to resemble Santa's beard. Ho, ho, ho!

Duplicate on green construction paper.

leaf

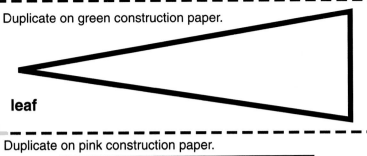

Duplicate on pink construction paper.

©TEC

face

Duplicate on white construction paper.

eyes

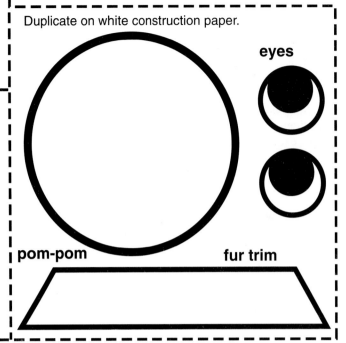

pom-pom   **fur trim**

Duplicate the cap and nose patterns on red construction paper.

nose

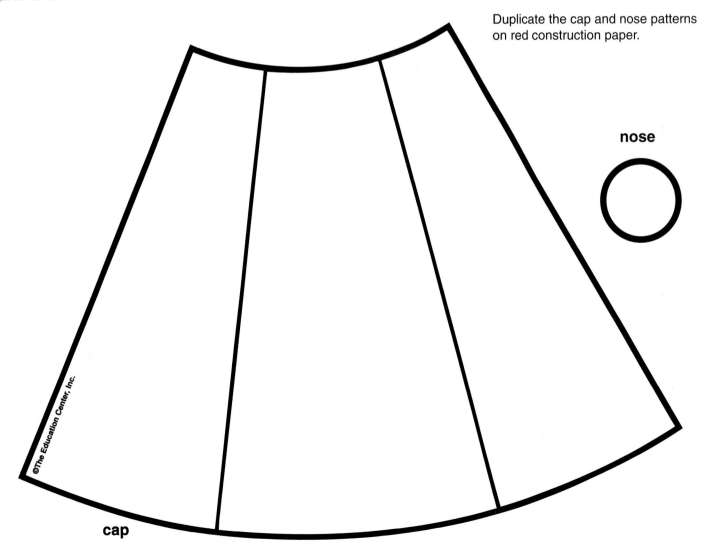

©The Education Center, Inc.

cap

Winter ❄❄

Christmas Carolers

Freestanding choir members make a festive holiday tabletop (or windowsill) display. One glance at these carolers and there's no doubt you'll be hearing the cheerful sounds of Christmas music.

For each choir member you will need:
tagboard duplicate of the face and hand patterns on page 58
12" x 18" sheet of red construction paper
4" x 12" piece of red construction paper
4" x 5" piece of black construction paper
5" x 8" piece of white construction paper
scissors
glue
stapler
tape
glitter pen (optional)

Steps for assembly:

1. **For the singer's body,** trim the large red rectangle as shown.
2. Bend the resulting half-circle into a cone shape and staple in place. Snip one-inch slits on opposite sides of the cone top as shown.
3. **For arms,** fold and trim the small red rectangle as shown.
4. Glue a hand cutout to each arm; then tape arms to the cone seam as shown.
5. **For songbook,** fold the black rectangle and tape to the palm of each hand as shown.
6. **For collar,** fold and cut the white rectangle as shown. Unfold and cut a triangular wedge from one side. Place the collar atop the cone.
7. Insert the face pattern. Fold under the triangular bit of the cone at the neck.
8. If desired, add glitter decorations to completed project.

Step 1

Step 2
slits
back of cone
staples

Step 3

Step 4
back

Step 5
front

Step 6

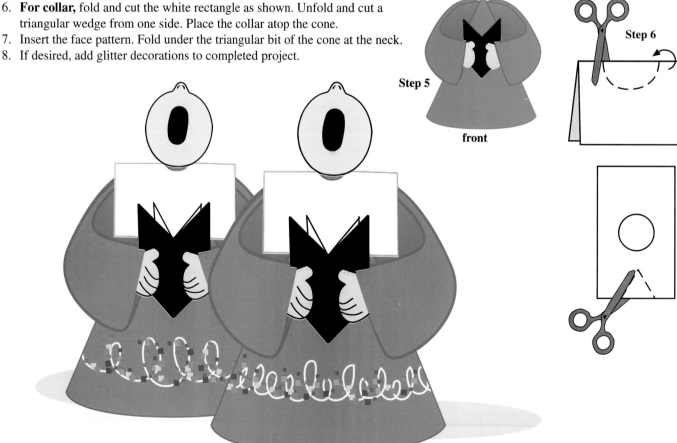

Finished Project

Silver And Gold Forest

Create the illusion of twinkling Christmas trees using metallic crayons. In advance, have your students donate silver, gold, and copper crayons. Create tree-shaped tagboard cutouts using the patterns on page 58. Cut black bulletin-board paper into 8" x 10" sheets (one per student). Place a tree-shaped cutout beneath a sheet of black paper and rub the paper with a metallic crayon. Move the cutout to another location beneath the paper and rub again. Repeat until the page is filled with overlapping tree designs. Add decorations to each tree using contrasting metallic crayons.

Toy Soldiers

For an eye-catching hallway or bulletin-board display, position these prim and proper soldiers shoulder to shoulder. Advance preparations are necessary for this project, and students must listen carefully to the directions for assembly. But the payoff for your efforts is big, bold, and beautiful!

Construction paper needed for each toy soldier:

7" x 12" piece of blue	a 2" tan circle
7" x 10" piece of red	a 3" black circle
two 2" x 9" pieces of red	two 1" pink circles
5" x 7" piece of tan	
5" x 7" piece of black	**Additional supplies:**
2" x 5" piece of black	scissors, glue, tape
two 2" squares of yellow	a black marker
yellow, red, and green for decorations	glitter (optional)

Steps for assembly:

1. **For the soldier's legs,** fold the blue rectangle in half and trim near the fold as shown. Unfold.
2. **For feet,** cut the black circle in half. Glue each half to the bottom of one leg.
3. **For chest,** glue the large red rectangle to the legs cutout.
4. **For arms,** glue the small red rectangles to the sides of the chest.
5. **For hands,** cut the tan circle in half. Glue each half to the bottom of one arm.
6. **For face,** fold and cut the tan rectangle as shown. Unfold and glue it atop the chest. For cheeks, glue on the pink circles. Add a smile and nose with black marker.
7. **For hat and brim,** fold and trim the black rectangles as shown. Unfold cutouts. Tape the smaller cutout (brim) to the larger cutout (hat).
8. **For shoulder ornaments,** fold and trim the yellow squares as shown and glue atop the arms.

Further decorate the soldier using yellow, red, and green paper and glitter.

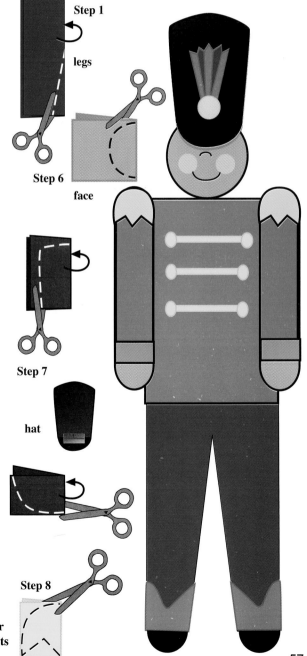

Step 1

legs

Step 6

face

Step 7

hat

Step 8

shoulder ornaments

Patterns

Use face and hand patterns with "Christmas Carolers" on page 56.

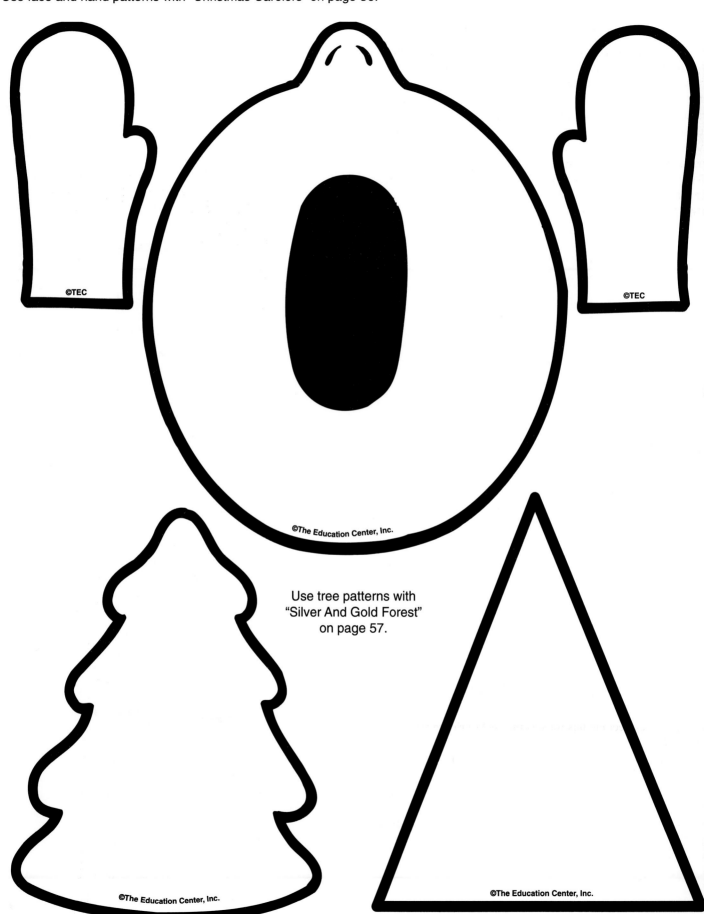

©TEC

©TEC

©The Education Center, Inc.

Use tree patterns with
"Silver And Gold Forest"
on page 57.

©The Education Center, Inc.

©The Education Center, Inc.

Frame It Festively

Highlight student artwork, original poetry, or holiday greetings with this festive frame. Purchase precut mats, or cut mats from poster board. With green tempera paint and holly- or dreidel-shaped sponge cutouts, have students sponge-print the frames. Glue on red paper-punch circles or sequins for holly berries. Glue a small red construction-paper rectangle to each frame. Have students glue Alpha-Bits® atop the rectangle to spell the name of the person for whom the project is intended. Using rubber cement, attach the artwork or composition behind the frame and trim if necessary. Framed original writings or artwork are likely to become beloved keepsakes.

Sweet Temptations

As they make these candies, visions of sugarplums and other sweet goodies will be dancing in the heads of your youngsters. To introduce the activity, show students an assortment of wrapped candies, and discuss the colors, designs, and wrappings. To make a piece of candy, glue two paper plates together, forming a disk shape. Once the glue has dried, paint the exposed surfaces of the plates to resemble a piece of candy. When the paint is dry, use plastic wrap to wrap the plates so that they look like wrapped candies. Use monofilament line to suspend each youngster's candy creation from the ceiling.

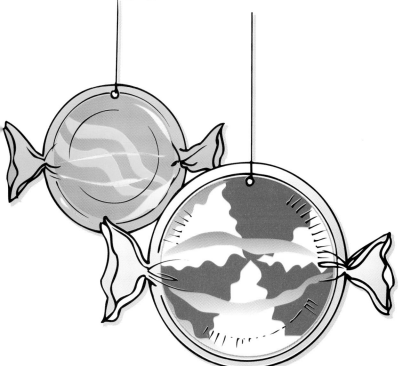

Jug-Top Christmas Trees

Youngsters will be delighted with these evergreen trees made with gallon-size jug lids. Collect jug lids for several weeks prior to this project. You will need ten lids per tree. Provide a tree tracer which will accommodate ten lids. To make a tree, trace the tree pattern onto green tagboard and cut out. To make ornaments for the tree, dip the top of each of ten lids into a shallow pan of glue and press it into a shallow pan of glitter. When the glittered lids are dry, dip each lid rim in a pan of glue before pressing it onto the tagboard tree cutout. Twist a small, red, tissue-paper rectangle to create a bow. Glue the bow to the top of your tree. These Christmas trees will make great additions to your holiday bulletin boards.

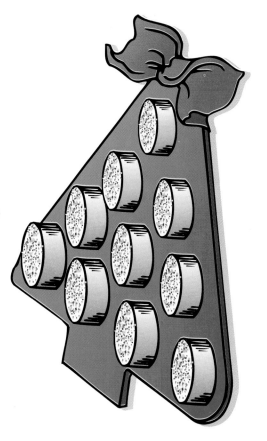

Winter ❄ ❄

Winter Watercolor

Create a gallery of eye-catching holiday artwork with this quick watercolor technique. For a Christmas tree, practice making a single long stroke near the bottom of your paper with a watercolor-filled, soft, pointed brush. This stroke will be the widest part of the tree. From there use the brush to quickly make zigzagging lines that diminish in length as they near the top of the page. Clean and refill the brush before adding the tree trunk and before using the brush to add small droplets of watercolor for multicolored lights. Practice making this tree several times, if desired, before making your final version on art paper. Mount the artwork on contrasting paper.

Vary the use of this technique to create a bright dreidel. Begin by making one long angled stroke. Then make quick zigzag strokes, working downward at an angle to a point. Clean and refill the brush before making the post of the dreidel with a single stroke.

Pinecone Christmas Tree

These Christmas tree creations are going to be a definite hit with your youngsters. Prepare for this activity by dyeing or spray-painting small seashell-shaped pasta in several different colors. Begin by gluing a pinecone to a small paper plate. Allow the glue to dry. Then glue cotton batting or tufts of cotton balls around the base of the pinecone. Insert the prepared pasta pieces into the sections of the pinecone, gluing if necessary to hold the pasta in place. Spray the pinecone lightly with imitation snow and sprinkle it with glitter. Top the pinecone tree with a gold star. Glue package cutouts around the base of the tree to complete the project.

Glittering Angels

Set your room aglow with these cheerful cherubs. Spray-paint the bottom of a divided paper plate, if desired, before beginning this project. For eyes, attach two large foil stars to the biggest section of the plate bottom. With markers or paint pens, add a smile, rosy cheeks, and a nose beneath the eyes. For hair, crumple fringed construction paper or pull apart pastel cotton balls, and glue them in place. Spread glue on each remaining section of the plate. Sprinkle glitter onto the wet glue. Bend a pipe cleaner to make a halo. Then poke one end of the pipe cleaner through the back of the project at the hairline, and twist it to hold the halo in place.

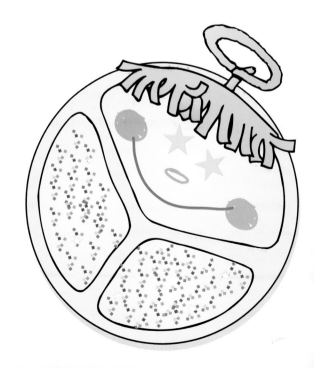

Menorahs And Christmas Trees

With paper loops and glue, youngsters can create bright, three-dimensional holiday artwork. And with their unmatched eye-appeal, you're going to love the festive holiday flair these projects bring to bulletin boards and classroom displays.

Menorah

For each menorah you need:
one 9" x 12" sheet of dark blue construction paper
ten 3/4" x 6" strips of yellow paper
eighteen 3/4" x 6" strips of light blue paper
nine 1 3/4-inch squares of yellow tissue paper
glue
diluted glue
paintbrush
pencil with eraser
clear or gold glitter

Steps:

1. For each of the 28 strips, glue one end atop the other end to form a loop.
2. For the menorah, center and glue two yellow loops horizontally at the bottom edge of the dark blue paper.
3. Center and glue another yellow loop above the first two.
4. Glue six yellow loops in a row above the last one.
5. Glue one yellow strip vertically above the center of the row.
6. To make each of the nine candles, glue two light blue loops vertically, one atop the other.
7. "Light" each candle by wrapping a tissue-paper square around a pencil eraser, dipping it in glue, and pressing it onto the top of the "candle."
8. Brush the yellow loops with diluted glue, and sprinkle on glitter.

Christmas Tree

For each tree you will need:
one 9" x 12" sheet of dark blue construction paper
fifteen 1" x 6" strips of green paper
two 1" x 6" strips of brown construction paper
glue
diluted glue
paintbrush
glitter

Steps:

1. For each of the 17 strips, glue one end atop the other end to form a loop.
2. Center and glue one green strip at the upper edge of the construction-paper sheet.
3. Working down the page, center and glue a row of two strips beneath the original one. Repeat with rows of three, four, and five loops.
4. Center and glue two brown strips vertically side by side for the tree trunk.
5. Add a cut-out star if desired.
6. Brush the green loops with diluted glue and sprinkle on glitter.

Winter ❄❄

"Berry" Best Ornaments

If you're nuts about inexpensive and attractive student-made ornaments, you're going to love these strawberries. To make a strawberry ornament, paint a walnut red using tempera paint. Allow to dry. To create the strawberry's seeds, first dip a toothpick in white tempera paint. Then repeatedly touch the toothpick to one side of the walnut to create small dots. Place the walnut, dotted side up, in an empty egg carton cup to dry before dotting the other side in the same manner. Use craft glue to attach green felt (leaves) and a green, looped, pipe cleaner section (stem) to the top of the walnut. Again the walnut may be placed in an egg carton cup while the glue dries. Then use a needle to pull thread through the felt leaves. Tie the thread off to make a hanger.

Personalized Holiday Ornaments

These large Christmas ornaments will add lots of sparkle and shine to your holiday room decor. Using a hole puncher, punch holes around the rim of an aluminum tart pan. Use silver tinsel garland to stitch in and out of the holes in the pan rim. Tie or tape the tinsel off and trim away the excess. Cut the center from a three-inch red construction-paper circle. Use glue and glitter to add some sparkle to one side of the resulting ring. Tape a photograph behind the ring before gluing it to the bottom of the pan. For a hanger, thread ribbon, yarn, or a silver pipe cleaner through the uppermost hole in the pan rim. Students' smiles beaming forth from a classroom evergreen are certain to set your classroom aglow with holiday warmth.

Bright, Lighted Christmas Trees

Warm your winter classroom with the bright glow of student-made trees. To make a tree, you will need one small brown rectangle and one green and one white construction-paper triangle of identical size. Using a variety of markers or crayons, completely color the white triangle in random fashion. Fold the green triangle (as shown) and cut or tear openings along the fold. Repeat this step several times. To complete your Christmas tree, glue the green triangle atop the white one, wedging a bit of the brown rectangle in between to create the tree's trunk. Display your trees in a window so that sunlight will set them aglow.

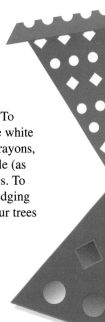

Colorful Holiday Greetings

Spread the Christmas spirit with these holiday greetings. In large block letters, have each student write a holiday word. Using red and green crayons, students color and decorate each letter uniquely. Including an occasional sprig of holly and bow adds to the effect. To complete the project, students cut around the letters and glue the words to red or green sheets of construction paper.

63

Winter ❄ ❄

Seasonal Chalk Stencils

You can chalk up this stenciling project as a seasonal favorite! Choose a simple, symmetrical, seasonal shape such as a dreidel, a tree, or a bell. Fold in half three different-sized tagboard pieces; then sketch and cut half of the shape from the fold of each piece. Unfold the tagboard pieces. To use each stencil, apply a thick layer of chalk to its inside edge. Place the stencil atop a sheet of construction paper; then, using a tissue, stroke the chalk into the cut-out area. Continue in this manner until the desired number of shapes result on the construction paper. Then carefully fold the chalked paper in half and cut half of the chosen shape from the fold. Unfold and mount the cutout atop a construction-paper sheet of a contrasting color. Trim the contrasting paper to within one-half inch of the cutout.

Gingerbread Houses

Your recycling enthusiasts are going to love making these gingerbread houses! To begin, cut a panel from a plain, brown grocery bag. Use white tempera to paint the outline, door, window(s), and trim of the house. When the paint has dried, add colorful details using chalks, crayons, or markers. To complete the house, cut around the outline; then cut along two sides of the door so it can be folded open. Showcase the gingerbread houses on a display entitled "Home Sweet Home." Behind the door of each house, attach a small snapshot of its residing artist.

Noteworthy Ornaments

Here's a festive project that students will be proud to give as holiday gifts. For each ornament, use a photocopier to reduce two pages of Christmas music to approximately 5" x 7" each. To "age" the carols, blot each using a damp tea bag. When dry, roll each carol into a tight tube and fasten its loose edge with a dab of glue. Glue the "scrolls" together side by side. Tie a length of red ribbon around the scrolls; then fashion a bow from the ribbon ends. Attach a sprig of holly and an ornament hook to complete the project.

Hearty Santa Placemats

Ho! Ho! Ho! You'd better watch out—Santa's on his way! Once these placemats are completed, students can "do lunch" with Santa on a daily basis. Or, if desired, the placemats can be saved for a special holiday party. If your students can't bear the thought of soiling Santa, mount the completed projects on a bulletin board for a jolly display.

Steps:

1. From one pink, one red, and one white sheet of 12" x 18" construction paper, cut large hearts of equal size.
2. To make Santa's face and beard, cut a medium-size heart from the white heart. Then glue the resulting "heart border" atop the pink heart.
3. To make Santa's hat, cut away the pointed section of Santa's face; then mount the face cutout atop the red heart as shown.
4. For the hatband, fold and trim a 3" x 9" strip of white construction paper as shown; then unfold and glue the band to Santa's hat.
5. Glue on marker-embellished construction-paper eyes.
6. Cut a mouth, mustache, nose, eyebrows, and hat ball from scraps of red and white construction paper. Attach the features in the order listed.
7. For durability, laminate the completed project.

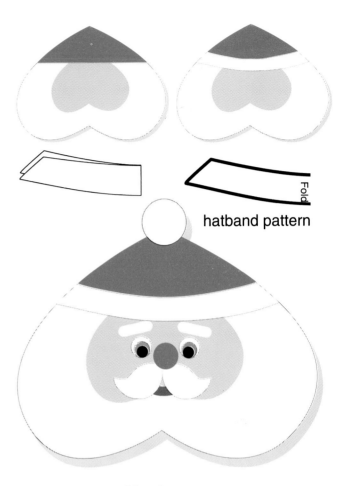

hatband pattern

Angelic Art

These adorable angels make a heavenly display! In advance, have each student bring a six-inch square of holiday gift wrap to school. From poster board, cut a six-inch equilateral triangle to use as a template. Then let the creating begin!

For each angel you will need:

a 6" square of holiday gift wrap
a 2" pink construction-paper circle
a 3" yellow construction-paper circle
two 1" yellow construction-paper circles
a 9" x 12" sheet of red, green, or blue construction paper
two quarter sections of an 8" gold doily

five pasta wheels
a black marker
foil stars
scissors
glue

Steps:

1. Trace the template onto the square of gift wrap. Cut out the triangle (body).
2. Glue the 1" yellow circles (feet) to the base of the triangle.
3. Mount the body and feet on the sheet of construction paper.
4. Glue the gold doily sections (wings) and the large yellow circle (halo) in place.
5. Using the marker, draw an angelic face on the pink circle. Glue the pink circle on the halo.
6. Attach the pasta wheels (hair) and foil stars.

Winter ❄ ❄

Christmas-Lights Garland

Deck the halls with these bright, colorful garlands! Duplicate the light patterns on page 67 on tagboard, one pattern per student. Provide each student with five sheets of 9" x 6" construction paper in various bright colors. Each child traces his pattern on the construction paper, making about five or six lights of each color. After cutting them out, he folds the lights on the dotted lines and glues them at one-inch intervals along a five-foot length of green yarn. For an added touch, attach a red paper bow at each end. Use the garlands to trim bulletin boards, windows, your chalkboard, and more!

Teardrop Ornaments

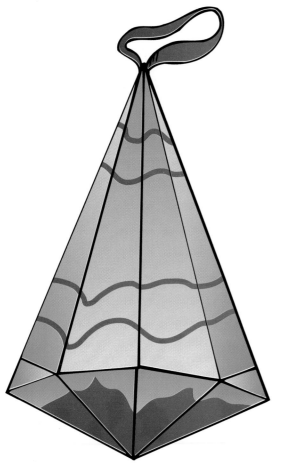

Have your students bring in old Christmas cards to make attractive, lasting ornaments. Duplicate the pattern on page 67 for each student to use as a run-through of the directions. When students understand the directions, have them cut out five-inch squares from their Christmas cards and follow the steps below.

Steps: (After each fold is made, reopen the paper before making the next fold.)
1. Fold A down to B. Crease.
2. Fold C over to D. Crease.
3. Fold the square diagonally, right bottom to the left top. Crease.
4. Fold the square diagonally, left bottom to right top. Crease.
5. Fold A down to meet diagonal X. Crease.
6. Fold A down to meet diagonal Y. Crease.
7. Fold C to meet diagonal X. Crease.
8. Fold C to meet diagonal Y. Crease.
9. Fold D to meet diagonal X. Crease.
10. Fold D to meet diagonal Y. Crease.
11. Fold B to meet diagonal X. Crease.
12. Fold B to meet diagonal Y. Crease.
13. Push center of paper downward while bringing four corners upward until they meet in a point. Tuck in the sides as you do this.
14. Loop a five-inch piece of curling ribbon and tie its ends together. Insert the knot in between the four corners of the paper. Use transparent tape to tape the four corners together.

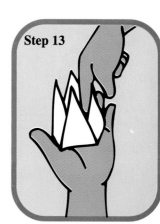

Step 13

Use with "Christmas-Lights Garland" on page 66.

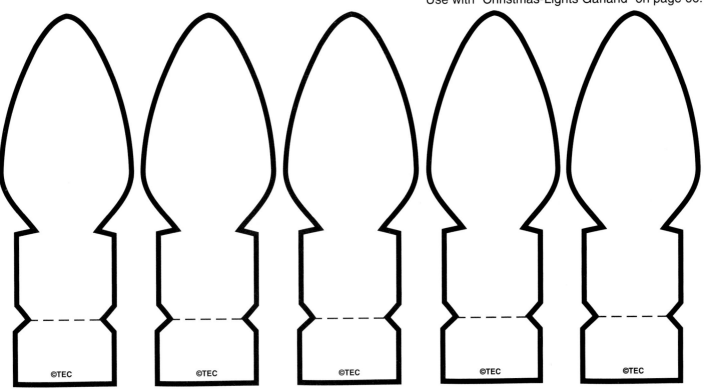

©TEC ©TEC ©TEC ©TEC ©TEC

Use with "Teardrop Ornaments" on page 66.

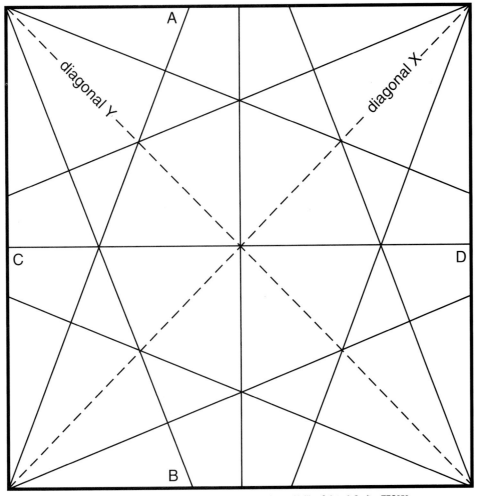

Winter ❄ ❄

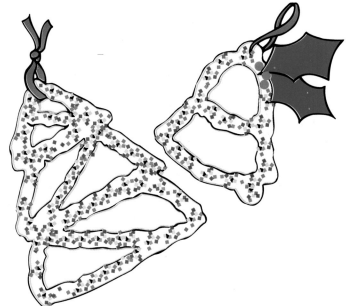

Razzle-Dazzle Ornaments

For a dazzling ornament that's fun to make, place a piece of waxed paper over a Christmas pattern. Trace the outline of the pattern with glue. Immediately sprinkle the glue with glitter and let dry overnight. When dry, gently peel the waxed paper away from the shape and add metallic thread for hanging. Students can add extra touches by dotting more glue on top of a dried shape and sprinkling with another color of glitter.

Christmas Card Ornament

Start this holiday project by asking students to donate old Christmas cards. Provide several sizes of circle patterns. Have each child locate a Christmas card with a festive scene. The student traces an appropriately sized circle pattern on the back of the scene. After cutting out the circle, the child cuts out a slightly larger ring from poster board. He then punches a hole at the top of the ring and circle and strings them together with a piece of yarn. For the finishing touch, have the student add glitter to the outer ring. Now that's a dazzling ornament!

Hanukkah Greetings

Give a cheer—the Festival Of Lights is here! Send Hanukkah greetings to loved ones with easy-to-make cards. On red construction paper, duplicate an enlarged copy of the pattern. Cut out and fold the card where indicated. Cut out two small, white rectangles (windows) and glue one to each card flap; then use fine-tipped markers to draw a Hanukkah scene inside each window. Add other details to the house using the markers, crayons, glue, and scraps of construction paper. Glue a small piece of notebook paper inside and write your holiday greetings. Great for Christmas greetings as well!

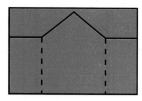

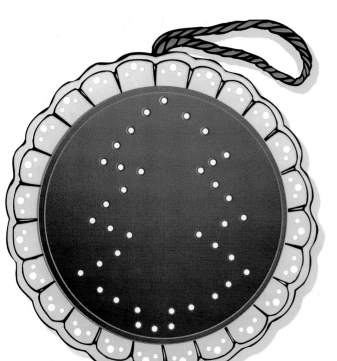

Punched-Tin Ornaments

These old-fashioned, punched-tin ornaments can be made quickly and easily. They look especially beautiful when placed directly in front of a Christmas tree light.

Materials needed include: hammers, small (not short) nails, lids from orange juice cans (the type with the plastic pull tab and no sharp edges), lace, glue, markers, and yarn.

Begin by drawing a simple design on the top side of the lid. Then punch evenly spaced holes on the design using a hammer and nail. Glue lace around the front edge. Add a piece of yarn on the back for hanging the ornament.

Paper Menorahs

Combine measuring skills and drawing to create these important symbols of Hanukkah. To make a menorah, use 9" x 12" construction paper, a ruler, a pencil, scissors, and markers.

Steps:

1. Measure and mark the 12-inch side of the sheet into thirds. Draw lines across the sheet.
2. On the top third of the sheet, measure and mark each inch along the 9-inch side. Draw lines so that this part is divided into nine equal rectangles.
3. Measure and mark one inch from the top and one inch from the bottom of this section. Draw lines across the sheet.
4. Draw a candle inside each rectangle. The shammash, the candle used to light the other candle, should extend beyond the other candles (see diagram). Color the candles' flames.
5. Carefully cut around the candles.
6. Bottom third of sheet: Fold the bottom edge of the paper up to the drawn line and crease. Fold up again at the drawn line and crease. Write a Hanukkah message on this part as shown. This third of the sheet can now stand in tentlike fashion.
7. To complete the project, fold down the top third of the sheet (the candles) so that it will stand.

Steps 1 and 2

9"

12"

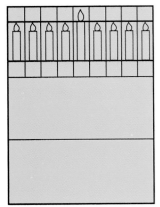

Steps 3 and 4

Step 5

Steps 6 and 7

Happy Hanukkah!

69

Winter ❄❄

Ho-Ho-Holiday Wreath

With just a little bit of crepe paper and time, your students can create lovely wreaths that will spread lots of holiday cheer! Cut a large supply of 2" x 2" squares from red and green crepe paper. Have each student trace a large circle onto tagboard. After cutting out the circle, the child cuts out the center to make a wreath. He then draws three small circles on the wreath for the red holly berries. The student wraps a piece of red crepe paper around the eraser end of a pencil, dips it in glue, and applies it to a circle. After filling the three circles with red crepe paper, the same method is used to fill in the remainder of the wreath with green crepe paper. Add pretty crepe-paper bows or ribbon to the wreaths. For an eye-catching display, mount the finished projects together on a bulletin board in the shape of a giant wreath. Because this project takes some time, it's the perfect solution to the holiday wiggles—just let your students work on the wreaths after they've completed their regular classwork.

Seasonal Plates

Don't toss those disposable microwave plates—transform them! Draw and color a picture on a plate using permanent markers. Glue ribbon or lace around the plate rim using craft glue. For a hanger, tape an open paper clip to the back of the plate. Label and date the artwork using a permanent marker. Voilà! A plate that was destined for the trash heap becomes a treasured family keepsake.

1st fold   2nd fold

3rd fold

cut

Snowflakes On Windowpanes

A blizzard of snowflakes obstructs the view from these waxed-paper windowpanes. Fold several squares of white paper and cut to create snowflakes. Press the snowflakes between two sheets of waxed paper using a warm, protected iron. Fold a 9" x 12" sheet of black construction paper in half vertically; then fold vertically again, pressing the folds to flatten. Fold the paper once again—horizontally this time. Using scissors with a good cutting edge, trim away a rectangular area as shown. Unfold and flatten the paper. Staple it to the waxed-paper-encased snowflake design, and trim away the excess waxed paper. Suspend these winter windowpanes from the ceiling or attach them to classroom windows.

The Old Silk Hat

Have each student decorate Frosty's old silk hat with holiday designs. Create a hat-shaped tagboard cutout using the pattern on page 72. Trace the shape onto black paper and cut out. Using construction-paper scraps, sequins, and miscellaneous craft supplies, decorate Frosty's hat with an original design. Glue on generous glitter outlines for a magical touch. "Thumpity, thump, thump. Thumpity, thump, thump. Look at Frosty go. Thumpity, thump, thump. Thumpity, thump, thump. Over the hills of snow!"

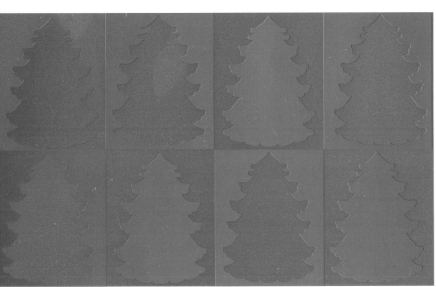

Positive/Negative Designs

This creative, paper-cutting technique yields interesting designs, perfect for all types of holiday decorating. Provide each student with two different-colored sheets of construction paper: one 12" x 18" and one 9" x 12".

Steps:
1. Fold the 9" x 12" sheet into fourths.
2. Draw the simple outline of a shape on the folded paper.
3. Carefully cut out the shape (without cutting into the sides). To make this step easier, use a pushpin to poke a hole or two through the folded paper on the outline. This will give you a starting place at which to begin cutting.
4. Unfold the paper. Cut into four sections along the fold lines.
5. Use the four borders and the four shapes to create a positive/negative design on the 12" x 18" sheet of paper.
6. Glue the eight pieces to complete the project.

Pattern

Use with "The Old Silk Hat" on page 71.

©The Education Center, Inc.

Snow Mobiles

The forecast is for winter blizzards with these enchanting snow mobiles.

Materials:

8 1/2" x 11" white paper	string or thread	yarn
12" x 2" strip of tagboard	scissors	hole puncher
glue	stapler	

Steps:

1. Cut two pieces of paper in half lengthwise. Each resulting piece makes one snowflake.
2. Fold one piece into 1/2" accordion pleats.
3. Cut a notch on each long side at the center as shown.
4. Double a four-inch piece of string. Tie it securely around the folded paper at the notches.
5. Make a variety of cuts on all sides of the folded paper.
6. Run a line of glue along one outside pleat. Place the end of a piece of string in the glue; then gently pull the snowflake open and sandwich the thread between the two outside pleats. Glue the opposite outside pleats together.
7. Make three more snowflakes in the same manner. Staple the ends of the tagboard strip together to form a circle. Punch four holes in the circle near the bottom; then attach four snowflakes.
8. Punch three holes at the top, add string or yarn, and hang.

   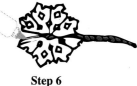

| **Step 2** | **Step 3** | **Step 4** | **Step 5** | **Step 6** |

Peppermint Scents

Turn your classroom into a sweet-smelling candyland! For fun, treat students to some real peppermint candy while they work. Hang finished projects in a hallway or in your room. Not only will the spirit of Christmas be present—but the scent as well!

Materials:

two white paper plates	red paint	paintbrush
plastic wrap	yarn	four to six cotton balls
pencil	hole puncher	peppermint extract
stapler		

Steps:

1. Draw a large X on the back of each plate; then draw a third line through each X.
2. Paint red alternating sections of each plate.
3. After drying, staple the plates together, leaving an opening.
4. Dip the cotton balls in peppermint extract; then wrap them in a small piece of plastic wrap (so the extract won't soak into the plates).
5. Place the cotton balls inside the plates. Staple the opening shut.
6. Tear off two pieces of plastic wrap, each about 12 inches longer than the plates. Sandwich the plates between the two pieces of plastic wrap. Twist the ends and tie with yarn.
7. Punch a hole in the top of the project, add a length of yarn, and hang.

Winter ❄ ❄

Shiny Snow Scenes

For a quick and easy winter art activity, glue a piece of aluminum foil onto a sheet of construction paper or tagboard. Cut white fabric scraps (or paper) and glue them on the foil to create a wintry snow scene. Add touches of glitter to give a frosty effect. Trim the finished picture with scrap lace or paper doilies cut to make a scalloped border. What a winter wonderland!

Snow Creations

Recycle plastic six-pack holders into beautiful, hanging decorations that can be enjoyed throughout the winter season. Begin collecting plastic holders two or three weeks prior to project day; it takes a matching set of 16 to make one decoration. For best results, divide students into pairs and have each pair work together to complete the project.

Steps:
1. Fold a plastic six-pack holder in half lengthwise. Staple point A to point B. Staple point C to point D.
2. Repeat Step 1 with the other 15 holders.
3. Staple point F of a holder to point E of a second one. Also staple point H of the first holder to point G of the second one. Staple a third holder to the second in the same manner. Continue stapling until you make a chain of eight holders.
4. In the same manner, staple the first and last holders of the chain together to form a circle.
5. Repeat Steps 3 and 4 to make a second circle with the eight remaining plastic holders.
6. Place the flat, rounded sides of the circles back to back, aligning them at the eight points. Staple together at point I (around the outside of the circles).
7. Attach a length of ribbon or yarn at point I.
8. Spray with artificial snow and hang for all to enjoy. For Valentine's Day, add pink and red hearts. In the spring, add yellow centers to make the decorations look like flowers.

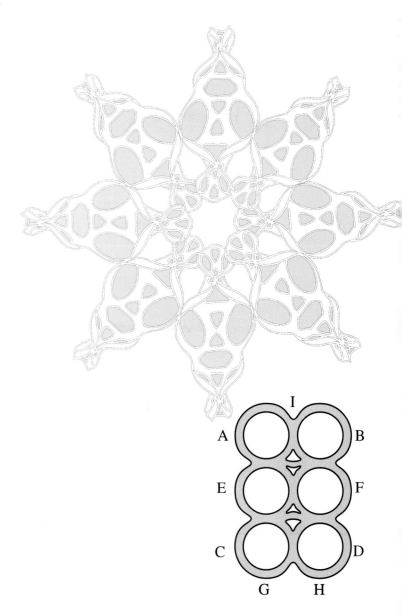

Oh, What A Snowman!

Children love to make these snowmen using circular hole reinforcements. To make a snowman, draw or trace a snowman outline onto light blue construction paper. Then attach hole reinforcements to cover the outline. Use construction-paper scraps and/or markers to make the snowman's hat, nose, eyes, mouth, arms, buttons, and scarf. "Thumpity, thump, thump. Thumpity, thump, thump. Look at Frosty go!"

Please Feed The Birds

Once your youngsters have created this bird-feeder art, they'll surely remember to feed their feathered friends. Begin by gluing a large, black construction-paper triangle near the top of a 9" x 12" sheet of construction paper. Then glue on three 1" x 2 1/2" and one 1" x 8" black paper strips to finish the bird feeder. Generously glue the feeder's perch and add a dab of glue at the bottom of the page. Sprinkle birdseed atop the glue. Cut out small paper red and blue birds, glue them on and under the feeder, and use crayons to add additional features to the birds. Folks will flock from all around to take a peek at these art projects.

Blizzards From Bubble Packaging

Your youngsters will bubble over with excitement when they see the results of this unusual painting technique. To begin, draw a winter scene on blue paper, omitting snow. Press a bubble-packaging sheet (bubble side down) onto a piece of foam rubber which has been previously coated with white tempera paint. Then press the bubble-packaging sheet onto the blue paper. Carefully remove the bubble packaging from the blue paper to reveal a unique snowy effect.

Winter ❄❄

Hole-Puncher Pictures

Put all those tiny circles punched from paper to good use. Gather a lot of paper circles that have been made with a hole puncher. Glue these circles to construction paper to make snow scenes. Whether your students are creative and plan a scene, or just dab the paper punches on randomly, you'll get unique scenes with various perspectives.

Paper-Chain Snowman

In December my reading lab students made white paper chains and stored them in garbage bags over the holidays. In January when students returned to school, we made a snowman for our hallway. We first stuffed two large garbage bags with crumpled newspaper for the body. A small plastic bag, also stuffed with newspaper, was used for the snowman's head. Students wrapped the chains around the bags to form the snowman; then they added black construction-paper eyes, a mouth, and a top hat. The carrot nose was a piece of orange construction paper shaped into a cone. A muffler of red felt fabric completed our snowman. My students love being greeted each day by our snowman!

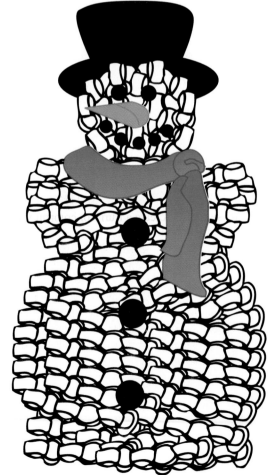

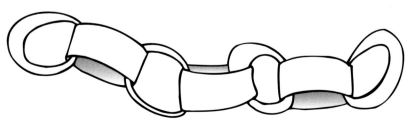

Twinkle, Twinkle

Set your room aglow with these dazzling masterpieces. Each student will need twelve 1" x 12" strips of construction paper and glue to make a star. To begin, fold each construction-paper strip into fourths (Step 1). Next unfold each strip and refold it into a triangle (Step 2). Secure each triangle shape by gluing together the two overlapping sections. Then arrange the shapes to form a six-pointed star and glue them together. When dry, brush the outer surface of the star with diluted glue and sprinkle it with glitter. Suspend the glimmering stars from lengths of monofilament line for a star-studded display.

Step 1   Step 2

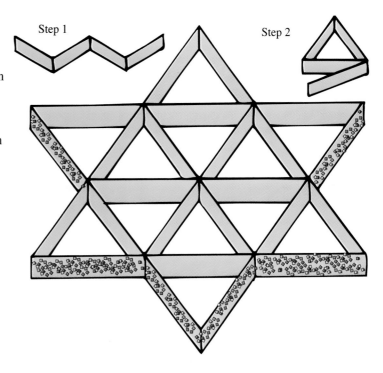

Snow Pals

Some paper, paint, sponge squares, and Q-tips® are all your youngsters will need to create these snowy pals. First sponge-print the lower third of a sheet of blue construction paper using white tempera paint. Next print the head and body sections of a snow pal and a smattering of snowflakes using a Q-tip® which has been repeatedly dipped in white paint. When the paint is dry, use the same technique to print colorful facial features, arms, mittens, a hat, a scarf, and other desired details.

Snowflakes From Filters

Follow these steps to create a flurry of colorful flakes! For each snowflake, first flatten a coffee filter. Fold the filter in half; then fold the resulting shape into thirds as shown. Create a desired snowflake design by snipping the sides, top, and bottom of the folded filter. Next dip portions of the folded filter into various colors of diluted food coloring. Gently squeeze to remove the excess water; then unfold and allow the filter to dry. For a shimmery effect, carefully brush the flakes with diluted glue; then sprinkle them with clear glitter. Mount the completed flakes on a bulletin board or suspend them from the ceiling on lengths of monofilament line. Let it snow!

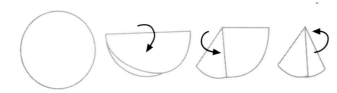

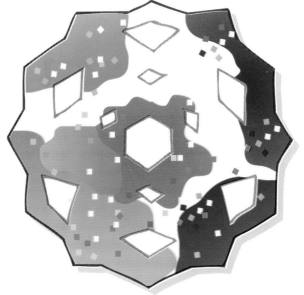

Winter ❄❄

Pompous Penguins

When displayed together, these pompous penguins will be a spectacular winter sight. In advance prepare a five-inch, an eight-inch, and a nine-inch circular tracer. For each penguin also gather two 3" x 9" strips of black construction paper, two 3" x 2" strips of orange construction paper, two 1 3/4-inch white paper circles, a small orange triangle, and a one-foot length of ribbon. Trace the eight-inch circle onto white paper and cut on the resulting line. Trace the five-inch and the nine-inch circles onto black paper and cut them out. Cut the black strips to resemble penguin wings, and round the orange strips to resemble penguin feet. Assemble the penguin as shown. For a fun writing activity, write a penguin story on the bird's belly!

Wintry Mobile

It's going to look like a blizzard in your classroom when each youngster hangs one of these mobiles! Using a variety of construction materials, create and decorate two two-sided cutouts, such as a mitten and a snowman. Decorate the right sides of each cutout pair, before gluing them wrong sides together and wedging a length of yarn between the sides. Also cut two snowflakes from folded paper. Punch a hole in each snowflake and attach yarn. Punch eight holes as shown in a 20" x 3" strip of tagboard. Decorate the tagboard as desired. Tie the loose yarn end from each of your cutouts into a hole along one side of the tagboard. Bend the tagboard strip ends to meet, and staple them in place. To suspend the mobile, thread and knot yarn lengths in the remaining holes; then tie the yarn ends around a plastic ring.

tagboard example

Garland Galore

If you're into recycling, you're going to love these decorative garlands made from grocery bags. To make a teddy bear, gingerbread man, or reindeer garland, make a tracer using the selected pattern on page 80. Cut a 15" x 4" strip from a large brown paper grocery bag. (From one bag, you can cut six strips of this size.) Accordion-fold the strip every three inches. Trace the design onto the folded strip. Cut on the lines and unfold. Decorate your teddies with twisted tissue-paper bows and facial features drawn with markers. Put the icing on your gingerbread men using paper-punch dots and markers, and put the glean in your reindeers' eyes and the shine on their noses with paper-punch dots.

Make a garland of snowmen using the pattern on page 80 and large white paper bags. Cut and decorate the snowmen similarly to the garlands described above. Then top off your snowmen with a black hat garland. Look at Frosty go!

Try these garlands as tree trimmers and bulletin-board borders.

Thumpity, Thump, Thump!

Well, Frosty said he'd be back again someday. And you can help him live up to that promise. To make a snowman suitable for suspending from the classroom ceiling, you will need: two paper plates, two 9" x 12" sheets of black construction paper, two 4" x 7" rectangles and two 1" x 7" bands of fabric or tissue paper, orange construction paper, glue, scissors, stapler, thread, and a hole puncher. Begin by gluing the paper plates rim-to-rim. Cutting through both thicknesses of the black paper, cut a top hat shape. Glue the hat cutouts together, sandwiching some of the paper plates between the cutouts. Using torn black paper scraps, glue "coal" eyes and mouth on both paper plate bottoms. Complete the snowman's faces with torn orange paper noses. Pinch and staple the middle of each 4" x 7" fabric or tissue-paper rectangle, and staple them back-to-back at the lower edge of the paper plates. Glue a fabric or tissue-paper band to each side of the hat, and trim to fit. Punch a hole near the top of the hat, and suspend the snowman using thread.

Patterns

Use with "Garland Galore" on page 79.

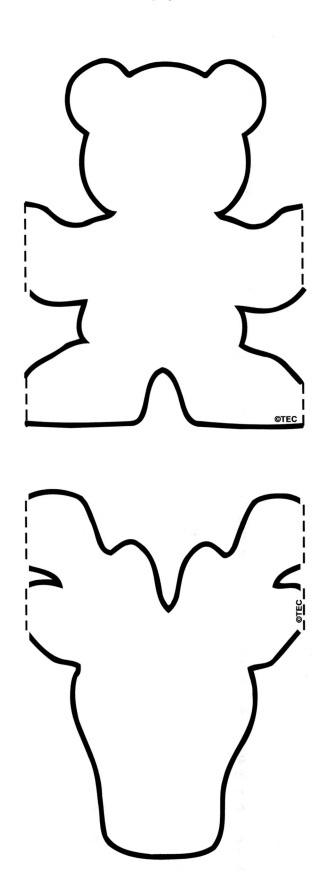

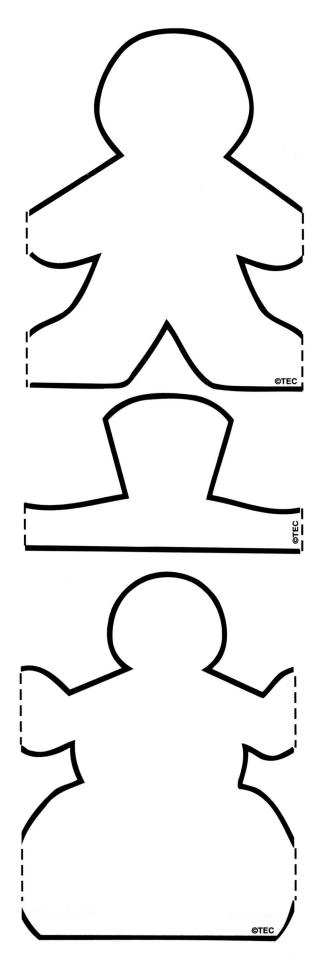

©TEC

Honest Abe

Celebrate Lincoln's birthday in style with this eye-catching presidential project.

To make the frame:
1. Fold and crease a 9" x 12" sheet of blue construction paper twice.
2. Place the oval frame template from page 82 on the folded paper as shown; then trace and cut on the resulting outlines.
3. Unfold the oval shape and glue it atop a 9" x 12" sheet of white construction paper.
4. Trim the white paper to within 1/8 inch of the outside of the oval.

To make Lincoln's face:
1. Fold a 5" x 7" black construction-paper rectangle in half (to 2 1/2" x 7").
2. Place the face template from page 82 on the folded paper as shown; then trace and cut on the resulting outlines.

To assemble and complete the project:
1. Glue Lincoln's face inside the oval frame; then glue on marker-embellished, construction-paper facial features.
2. Using the star templates from page 82, trace and cut out the desired number of construction-paper stars. Mount the stars around the frame.
3. On the back, near the bottom of the frame, glue or tape several lengths of curling ribbon.
4. Punch two holes near the top of the frame. Thread a length of curling ribbon through the holes and knot it for hanging.

Valentine Wishes

Set hearts aflutter with these lacy valentine greetings.

Materials needed:

9" x 12" sheet of red construction paper	scissors
3/4" x 5" pink construction-paper rectangle	crayons or markers
8" circular doily	glue

Steps:
1. Fold the sheet of construction paper in half; then indicate the center of the fold with a crease.
2. Make a template using the pattern on page 82.
3. Trace the template twice onto the fold as shown.
4. Cut on each curved line; then fold down each cut edge and make a crisp crease along each resulting straight edge.
5. Open the paper fully. Pull each heart shape toward you; then fold the shapes to the inside as you close the card.
6. Open the card. The pop-up hearts (butterfly wings) should open when the card is opened. Make any necessary adjustments.
7. For the butterfly's body, trim the pink rectangle as desired; then glue it between the butterfly wings.
8. Add desired decorations and a valentine wish to the inside of the card using crayons or markers. Sign it; then close the card.
9. Fold the eight-inch doily in half. Glue the folded card inside the folded doily.
10. Add a valentine greeting to the outside of the card.

I Love You, Mom

Happy Valentine's Day!
Christina

Outside finished project

Step 1

Step 3

Step 4

81

Patterns

Use the oval frame, face, and star patterns with "Honest Abe" on page 81.

oval frame

face

Place on fold.

Place on fold.

Place on fold.

Place on fold.

Place on fold.

©TEC

©TEC

©TEC

©TEC

©TEC

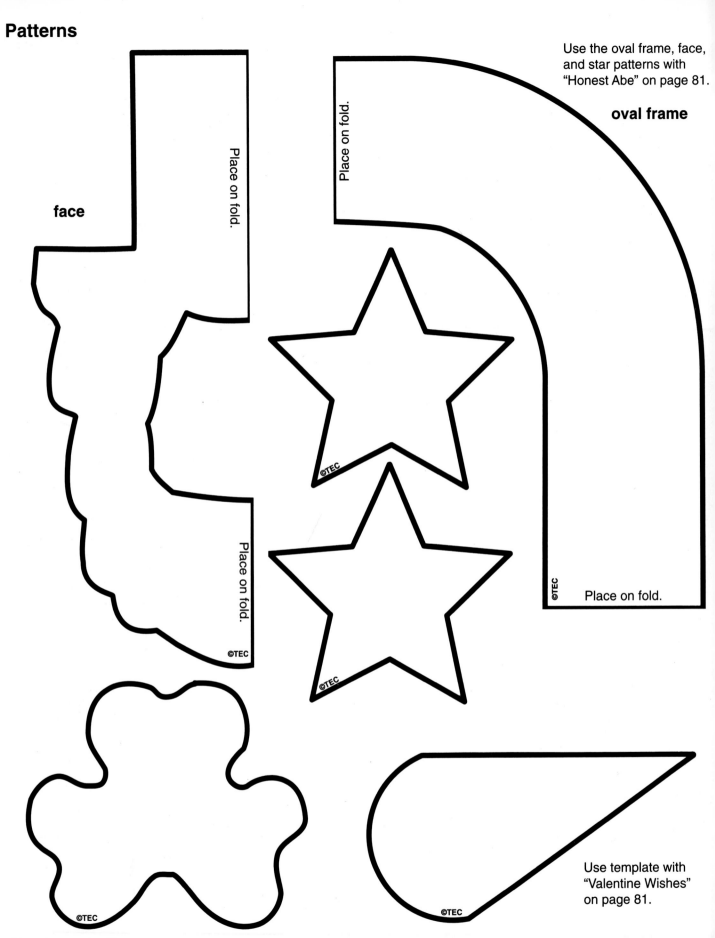

Use template with "Valentine Wishes" on page 81.

Use shamrock with
"Picturesque Shamrocks" on page 92.

©1995 The Education Center, Inc. • *The Best Of* The Mailbox® *Arts & Crafts* • TEC850

Say Cheese, George

By George, it's time for a presidential project! So guide your students in creating their own versions of our nation's first president. Use the pattern on page 90 to make a tracer; then trace the outline onto folded paper. Cut and glue this hat atop a white circle cutout glued to a sheet of yellow construction paper. Glue a half-circle (to match the hat) beneath the circle for George's jacket. Add quartered doilies for George's colonial ruffles. Using markers or crayons, add facial features. Glue a tuft or two of cotton balls or cotton batting to mimic a stately powdered wig.

Valentine Abstracts

Listen carefully—you just may hear a heartbeat or two when you display these valentine projects! Give each student a 12" x 18" piece of art paper. Have the child use a pencil to lightly draw several large heart shapes (the bigger, the better) on his paper. Then have him draw three intersecting lines, each going from one edge of the paper to another. To finish the project, let the student select three colors of paint to use, along with black paint and white paint. Have the student paint the sections of his abstract. Encourage your young artists to not only use the white and black paints to fill in the areas but also to mix them with the other colors to create different hues and shades. After the paintings have completely dried, let students outline the painted areas with a bright marker. Mount each drawing on a piece of red or pink construction paper to display it. Use this activity with shamrocks in March!

Valentine Lovebirds

If you're looking for a quick and easy valentine project, these lovebirds are singing your tune! Cut a supply of pink and red construction-paper strips, all the same size. Curl both ends of one strip by wrapping them around a pencil. Curl only one end of three more strips. Staple the strips together as shown to make a curly lovebird. Make several birds in the same way, using different colors and lengths of strips; then hang them from the ceiling or use them to make a Valentine's Day mobile. How "tweet" it is!

Winter ❄ ❄

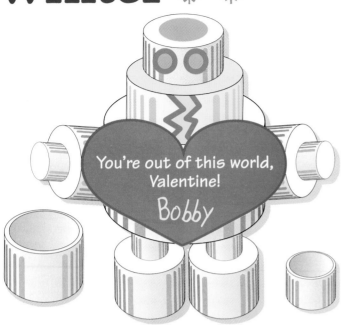

You're out of this world, Valentine!

Bobby

Valentine Aliens

For an out-of-this-world valentine that also encourages recycling, try this fun project. Save plastic lids from spray cans and screw-on bottle caps. Tape the lids and caps together to form a figure. Glue on two or three layers of torn-paper strips. After the last layer has dried, paint your alien and add paper features such as eyes or a mouth. For the finishing touch, label a paper heart with your valentine message; then glue the heart in place. How's that for a close encounter of the loving kind!

A Peek Into My Heart

What's inside your students' hearts this Valentine's Day? Find out by dividing your class into pairs. In turn, have each student lie down on a large piece of white bulletin-board paper; then have his partner trace the outline of his body onto the paper. After tracing, have each student color his outline to resemble himself, gluing on cut-paper features where desired. To finish the project, have each student cut out a large, red paper heart. Inside the heart, have the student add original drawings or magazine pictures and photos illustrating what is special to him. Have students glue the hearts to their body outlines; then have them cut out the bodies and display them on a large wall space.

Love's A-Blooming!

Send greetings to a loved one with a bloomin' special card! Place a large, tagboard heart pattern on a piece of folded construction paper so that the top of the heart touches the fold. Trace the heart onto the paper; then cut it out, making sure not to cut on the fold. On the front of the resulting heart-shaped card, glue pictures of bright-colored flowers cut from old seed catalogs, gift wrap, or magazines. After completely covering the front of the card with flowers, glue on letters naming the card's recipient. Write your message inside. Hallmark would be proud to display these creative cards!

Through And Through—
Red, White, And Blue

With Lincoln's birthday, Washington's birthday, and Presidents' Day just around the corner, it's time to be in an especially patriotic mood. Give students an opportunity to show their true colors with these hanging banners. To make a banner, glue three red and two white 20" crepe-paper streamers to the rim of a blue disposable plate, alternating the colors. Squeeze a trail of glue along the highest ridge of the plate rim. Invert another blue plate atop the first one, and allow the glue to dry. Decorate the exposed surfaces of the plates with star-shaped cutouts or stickers. Use a hole puncher to punch a hole in the plate rim opposite the streamers. Then attach a yarn length for suspending the banner.

Valentines With Va-voom!

These unusual valentine projects will make great surprises for students' loved ones. To begin, cut two identical heart shapes from transparent vinyl. (Upholstery shops sell this fabric.) With one cutout atop the other, use a hole puncher to punch evenly spaced holes around the edges. Using ribbon or yarn, lace through all but a few holes. Through this opening, insert conversation hearts (or other valentine candy), a handmade valentine, and one or two heart-shaped trinkets. Lace through the remaining holes, and tie and trim the loose ribbon or yarn ends.

This idea may be so popular with your youngsters that they'll want to create shamrock-shaped versions for St. Patrick's Day and egg-shaped versions for Easter. For an end-of-the-year surprise, make sandcastle-shaped versions filled with seashells and other treats to present to your youngsters on the last day of school.

Wings Of Love

You've heard of the wings of love. Well, now they can flutter into your classroom just in time for Valentine's Day. To make one of these butterflies, begin by stacking two 4 1/2" squares of paper. Fold the squares in half (one inside the other) and draw concentric half-heart outlines as shown. Cut on the lines you've drawn. (If two-toned butterflies are desired, trade both hearts of one size with someone who has cutouts of another color.)

Decorate each of the smaller heart cutouts. Position a larger heart "frame" atop each of the smaller cutouts so that the pointed heart bottoms meet. Glue or tape each pair at the points. Place the heart pairs with decorated sides together, and staple at the points. Spread the pairs apart and pin them to a bulletin board, so that they stand out like wings from the board. Fluttering around a display of student work, these butterflies can be quite eye-catching.

Winter ❄ ❄

Valentine Safari

If your students are wild about animals, February is the perfect time to create a bunch of wild-and-crazy critters. Before beginning, gather an assortment of art supplies, glue, construction paper, and several sizes of heart-shaped tracers. Trace and cut out one or more hearts. Glue it (them) to contrasting construction paper. Use a marker or crayons to convert the heart(s) into a wild animal. The more you use your imagination, the wilder your animals will be!

Touching Hearts

This valentine keepsake will touch the hearts of the parents, grandparents, or other loved ones of your youngsters. To make this keepsake, cut a half-heart shape from a folded piece of construction paper. Reserve the heart cutout for another activity (like "Valentine Safari" above). Glue the remaining heart-shaped paper frame to a piece of art paper. Press palms and fingers into a shallow pan of tempera paint; then press the paint-covered hands onto scrap paper before pressing them within the heart-shaped frame formed by the glued papers. When the paint has dried, personalize the paper and write "Hands that touch the heart…" across the top of the project.

Hands that touch the heart...

Love, Caroline

Sandpaper Prints

Making these prints is a uniquely tactile experience for your youngsters. To begin, use crayons to draw and color a seasonal design on a half sheet of coarse sandpaper. Press hard and color thoroughly as you work. Place the decorated sandpaper facedown on an identically sized sheet of art paper that is on several layers of newsprint. Place another sheet of newsprint on the sandpaper to protect your iron. Then press the papers with a warm iron to transfer the crayon drawings to the art paper. For display, glue the sandpaper and the print to a large sheet of construction paper or tagboard.

Sticky Shamrocks

Your little leprechauns are likely to love these peel-and-stick decorations they can make themselves. Tint glue with green food coloring or tempera paint. Mix well; then pour the glue into a squeeze bottle. (If you're short on time, use Elmer's GluColors™ instead of mixing your own.) Also, in preparation for this project, tape a shamrock design beneath a sheet of clear plastic. (Fast-food restaurants use clear take-out containers which have surfaces that are excellent for this.) Looking through the plastic, squeeze a trail of tinted glue atop the shamrock outline. Fill in the shamrock shape with glue. If desired, sprinkle small glittery beads or small sequins along the shamrock's edge. When the glue has thoroughly dried, peel it from the plastic. To use it as a decal, stick it to any slick glass, plastic, or metal surface. Or punch a hole in the dried glue, thread it with ribbon, and wear it as a necklace on St. Patrick's Day.

Shamrocks

You can almost smell the springtime air as you view these printed shamrock fields. You will need a portion of a sponge trimmed into the shape of a shamrock (without the stem). Dampen the sponge and clip a clothespin to one side for a handle. On light green paper, draw slender curving stalks with a green marker. Pour green tempera paint in a pan bottom. Dip the shamrock-shaped sponge into the paint (holding it by the clothespin), print shamrocks at the tops of the stalks on your paper, dry, and display.

High-Flyin' Fun

Creating kites is a breeze! Begin with a 7" x 5" cotton remnant. Clip the fabric at 1/2" intervals. Rip at each slit, creating several 7" x 1/2" strips of cloth. Trace a diamond shape on a 9" x 12" sheet of construction paper and cut out. Staple a colorful 24" long yarn or ribbon tail to each "kite." Tie fabric strips to the kite tail and trim off if necessary. All that ripping, tying, and cutting is great for your youngsters' motor skills, and the colorful kites make a lovely springtime display!

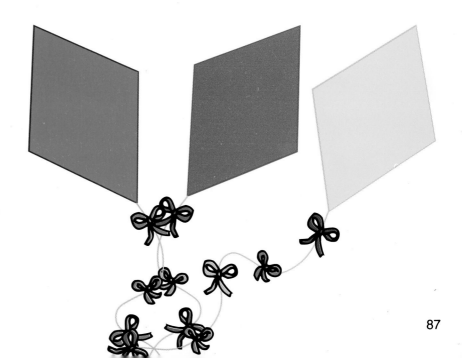

Winter ❄❄

A Good Luck Charm

Just in time for St. Patrick's Day, bedeck your classroom with showers of emerald shamrocks. For this project you will need three 12"-square samples of original artwork featuring the color green. Use a different medium (such as chalk, tempera paint, or watercolor) for each sample, if desired. (Any other green paper such as computer paper or gift wrap can be substituted for the artwork.) Make a half-shamrock pattern similar to the one shown. Cut out and place this pattern on a folded artwork square. (Fold the artwork to the inside.) Trace and cut out the design. Repeat this process with the remaining two pieces of artwork.

To assemble this project, place one folded shamrock cutout on a tabletop. Glue the upper paper surface. Lining up the edges, place another folded shamrock cutout atop the first one. Glue its upper paper surface, and place the remaining folded shamrock atop the second one. Attach several crepe-paper streamers or strands of curling ribbon to the exposed shamrock stem. When the glue is dry, pick up the folded shamrock cutouts and bend the top and bottom surfaces toward one another until they meet. Glue in place. Suspend the shamrock from monofilament line, and watch it dance and twirl in the springlike breezes of St. Patrick's Day.

Hoppy Holders

If you're hoping for a "toad-ally" new look for Valentine's Day this year, this valentine holder might just get you hoppin'. Begin by creating a tracer like the one shown. Trace this pattern onto a 12" x 18" sheet of green construction paper; then cut on the outline. Cut out, decorate, and attach white, construction-paper eyes. Complete the face by drawing on additional features. Cut another sheet of green construction paper into fourths as shown. Trim one end of each resulting strip for feet. Glue each of the untrimmed strip ends to the back of the body. From a 12" square of red construction paper, cut a heart shape. Attach the heart cutout to the body section of the frog so that it creates a pocket. Without folding the strips, curve them toward the valentine, and staple them in place. If desired, personalize the heart cutout and slip a bag inside it for holding valentines and treats. "Hoppy" Valentine's Day!

This idea can be modified to create other animal characters. For a bear, cut a head-and-body shape, attach ears and eyes, and draw facial features. Attach a heart cutout; then attach decorated paw cutouts.

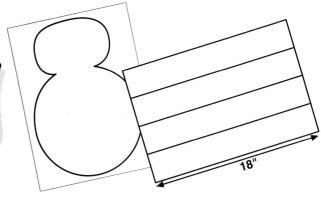

No More "Lion"...Baaaah!

No "lion"! "Ewe" and your students are going to love this art project. Using the patterns on page 90 as tracers, cut out a sheep's face, two ears, and two legs from black construction paper. Cut two, 1" white circles and two, 3/4" black circles for eyes. Glue the smaller circles atop the larger ones, and glue them to the sheep face cutout. Glue the face cutout to a thin, white luncheon-size paper plate, before gluing the ear cutouts to the back side of the plate. Glue the small plate to a larger plate as shown, and glue the legs to the back of the larger plate. "Ewe" will have conjured up everything but the "baaaah" when you add a fluffy cotton-ball tail to the top of the larger plate.

Irish Potatoes

Invite your students' creative shenanigans with Irish potato pairs. For each potato pair you will need 12" x 18" sheets of white and brown construction paper, a 9" x 12" sheet of green construction paper, and a 6" square of black construction paper. Cut two free-form potatoes from the brown paper; cut shamrocks from the green and a hat from the black. Then glue these pieces to the white paper in a unique and "a-peeling" way. Add comical facial expressions using black marker or crayon.

Irish Eyes Are Smiling

Invite the luck of the Irish with lovely, student-made shamrock wreaths. Cut away the center of a thin paper plate. Cover the rim of the plate with various shades of green shamrock cutouts. (Cut shamrocks from folded paper as shown.) Glue your picture to another shamrock cutout, and use string to suspend this shamrock from the rim of the plate. Add a bow to complete the wreath. Display these wreaths with the caption, "Irish Eyes Are Smilin'."

Rainbow Art

Set aside two art sessions to create this feast for the eyes. Use colored chalk to create a rainbow of color stripes, swirls, or geometric shapes on white art paper. Be careful not to smear the chalk. Spray the chalk art with a fixative such as aerosol hairspray. Later cut out a black silhouette or a grouping of silhouettes, and glue it (them) atop the chalk art. Now that's colorful art!

Patterns

Use sheep face, ear, and leg patterns with "No More 'Lion'…Baaaah!" on page 89.

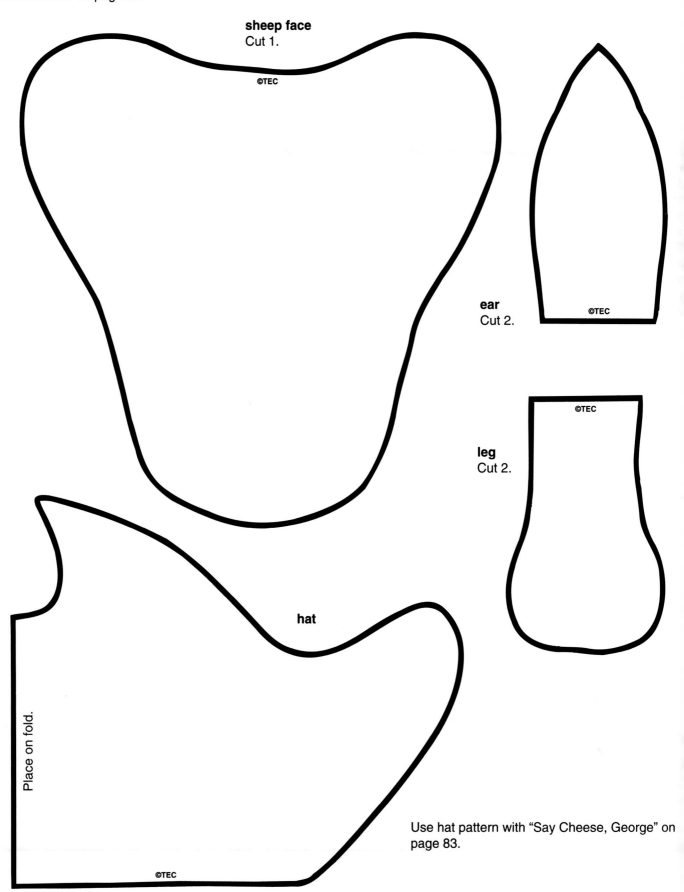

sheep face
Cut 1.

©TEC

ear
Cut 2.

©TEC

leg
Cut 2.

©TEC

hat

Place on fold.

©TEC

Use hat pattern with "Say Cheese, George" on page 83.

Shamrock Shenanigans

Think green for St. Patrick's Day. To make these shamrock works of art, you'll need a shamrock tracer and two octagonal tracers, one just a little larger than the other. Trace the smaller octagon onto a white sheet of paper and the larger one onto a green sheet of paper. Using the shamrock tracer and a green crayon, trace shamrock shapes onto the white paper, without overlapping the designs. Decorate each shamrock with a different design; then glue the white paper octagon to the green one. Glancing at these fields of green shamrocks may just put a little Irish lilt into your stride.

Shaggy Shamrocks

For St. Patrick's Day why not create some shamrock-inspired greenery? To begin, trace a shamrock outline onto a sponge; then cut out and place the sponge in a shallow dish. Generously sprinkle the sponge with grass seed and pour a little water into the dish. Keep the seeds moist, and before you know it, greenery will be cropping up all over the sponge.

Winter

Picturesque Shamrocks

Invite the luck of the Irish into your classroom with student-made shamrock greenery. Trim a portion of a sponge into the shape of a shamrock (pattern on page 82). Dampen the sponge and clip a clothespin to one side for a handle. Pour green paint into a pie tin. Holding the clothespin, dip the shamrock-shaped sponge into the paint. Then randomly print shamrocks onto a 9" x 12" sheet of yellow construction paper as shown. When the shamrocks are dry, use a green marker to draw a slender, curving stalk from each shamrock to a designated point at the bottom of the paper. To make a three-dimensional vase, fold under a 1/2-inch flap from each three-inch side of a 3" x 5" construction-paper rectangle. Position the rectangle atop the project as desired; then glue the flaps in place. Mount the completed project atop a slightly larger piece of black construction paper.

Kite Of A Different Color

No two kites will look alike when you use this inventive technique. On a large sheet of art paper, drizzle white glue randomly. A day later, prepare each paper for painting by misting it with water. Using watercolor paints, paint the paper. (Let the colors mingle to create unique effects.) When the painting is dry, trace a diamond shape onto the paper, then cut on the resulting outline. Tape a length of yarn to the back of the kite at one end.

To create an eye-catching kite tail, clip a five-inch cotton remnant square at 1/2-inch intervals; then rip at each slit to create several strips of cloth. Tie the resulting strips onto the kite tail. Creating these kites is a real breeze!

A Dandy Lion

Even if March doesn't roar in like a lion, your students will have ferocious fun making this project! Use a hole puncher to make a series of side-by-side holes around the entire rim of a yellow plastic bowl. Individually loop two six-inch lengths of brown yarn through each hole as shown. Trim the resulting mane as desired. Cut out and attach construction-paper ears and eyes. Glue on wrinkled, brown paper strips for whiskers; then attach a pink pom-pom nose. Use a permanent marker to draw the lion's mouth. For a fun literature tie-in, read aloud Don Freeman's book *Dandelion* while youngsters are completing their projects.

Let's Go Fly A Kite!

Spring is in the air, bringing with it the perfect opportunity to combine art with poetry writing. After discussing the often-changeable weather of spring, have each child write a poem about weather. Then feature those poems on colorful, handmade kites.

Kite-Making Steps:

1. Fold a sheet of newspaper in half; then roll it tightly to make a pole. Tape it securely at both ends and in the middle.
2. Repeat Step 1 to make a second pole.
3. Use string to tie the two poles together in the middle.
4. Beginning at one end of one pole, wrap and tape string to each end to form a kite shape.
5. Lay the kite frame on a piece of bulletin-board paper. Trace the kite shape, making your tracing larger than the kite frame.
6. Cut out the kite shape; then trim the four pointed ends slightly as shown.
7. Copy your poem on the kite cutout. Decorate your kite by gluing on construction-paper cutouts.
8. Lay the kite frame on the back of the kite cutout.
9. Fold the paper over the string on one side of the kite and tape it down securely. Repeat the process for the other three sides.
10. Add a kite string and a tail decorated with fabric-scrap ties. Now go fly your poetic masterpiece!

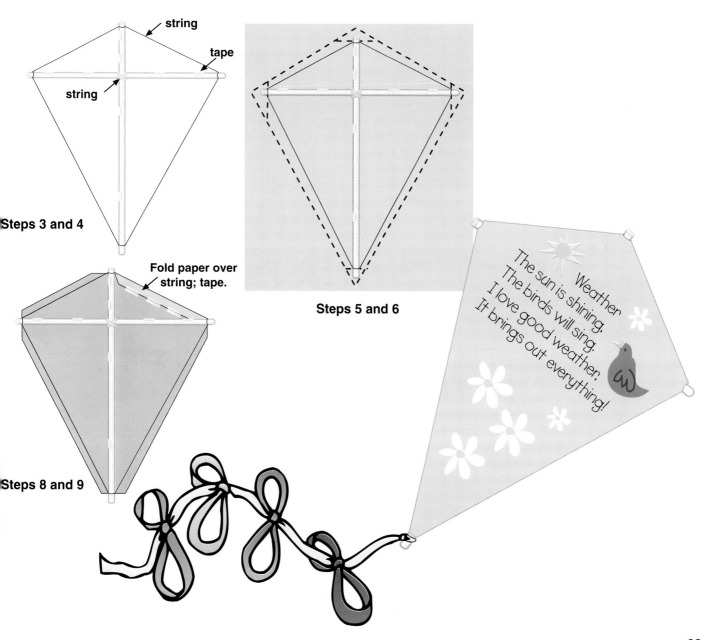

Steps 3 and 4

Steps 5 and 6

Steps 8 and 9

Fold paper over string; tape.

string

tape

string

Weather
The sun is shining.
The birds will sing.
I love good weather.
It brings out everything!

93

Spring

Tissue-Paper Butterflies

Make these butterflies in a flit and a flutter! To make a butterfly, cut out two construction-paper copies of the butterfly pattern on page 95. On one butterfly frame, squeeze a thin trail of glue around each cut-out area; then cover each area with a 3" x 3 1/2" piece of colorful tissue paper. Also attach two bent pipe-cleaner antennae. Next squeeze a thin trail of glue around the outer edge of the frame. Position the second frame atop the first, and align the two. When dry, trim away the overhanging tissue paper and your butterfly is ready to take flight!

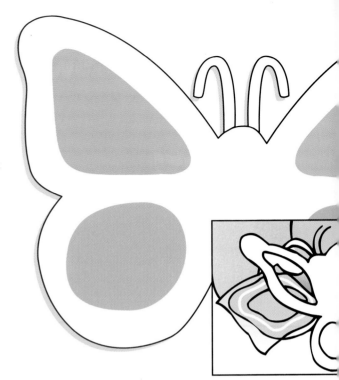

Quilled Butterflies

A display of these fancy fliers attracts lots of attention! To make a butterfly, cut out a tagboard tracer using the butterfly pattern on page 95. Also cut a supply of 6" x 1/2" strips of black construction paper. Using the tracer, cut a butterfly shape from colorful construction paper. One at a time, wrap each of several black strips around a pencil; then slide the strip off and glue it—standing on edge—to the cutout. Hold each "quilled" strip in place until the glue has dried enough to hold it. Continue in this manner until the cutout is filled in. When the project has dried, mount it atop another sheet of construction paper; then trim this paper to create an eye-catching border. Repeat this step a second time. Attach bent pipe-cleaner antennae and your project is complete. Now that's a fancy flier!

Folded Flyers

Your recycling enthusiasts are going to love making these eye-catching butterflies! To make a butterfly, tear two brightly colored pages from a discarded magazine. Fold one page in half; then trace the half-pattern on page 96 onto the page. Cut on the resulting outline—not on the fold. Next unfold the paper and refold it so that the rounded ends meet. Starting at the fold and working toward one rounded end, accordion-fold one-half of the pattern. Fold the remaining half of the pattern in the same manner; then set the piece aside. Next cut a 6 1/2-inch square from the second magazine page. Fold the square in half, making a triangle. Starting at the fold and working outward, accordion-fold one-half of the pattern. Fold the remaining half of the pattern in the same manner. Join the two folded pattern pieces with a length of black pipe cleaner as shown; then gently spread the wings of the butterfly. There you have it! A one-of-a-kind folded flyer!

©TEC

Patterns

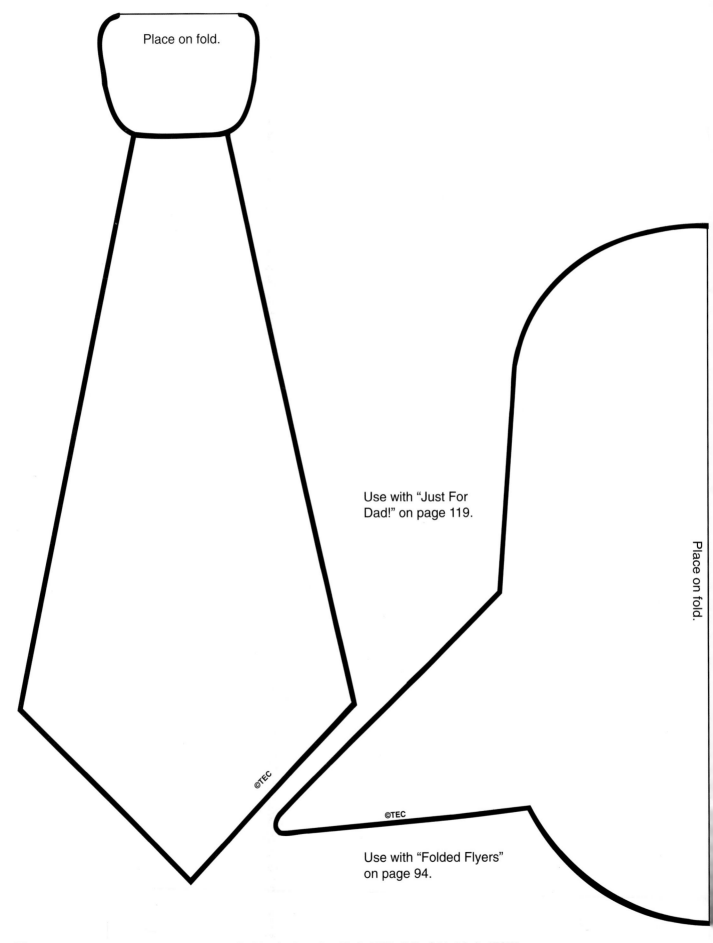

Place on fold.

Use with "Just For Dad!" on page 119.

Place on fold.

©TEC

©TEC

Use with "Folded Flyers" on page 94.

April Showers

Ducking under a bright umbrella can be a great way to wait out a typical spring shower. Begin by folding down the upper four inches of a sheet of art paper to create a flap. Draw an umbrella that is nearly as wide as the paper. Sketch it so that the top of the umbrella is near the fold and the tips of the ribs are near the bottom of the paper flap. Scallop the bottom of the flap along the umbrella bottom. Color the umbrella and the area around it on the flap. Then add a shower of raindrops on and around the umbrella. Lift the flap to draw and color yourself, the umbrella handle, the surrounding spring scenery, and lots and lots of raindrops.

Positively Perky Petals

Fill your classroom with these pretty posies for lots of springtime eye appeal. To begin making a flower, cut a 12" x 4 1/2" strip of green construction paper to resemble a flower's stem and leaves. Then color the center of a flattened muffin-tin liner. Place this liner atop two or three other flattened liners. Poke a brad through the muffin-tin liners and through the top of the paper stem. Spread the prongs of the brad to hold the liners in place. Cutting through all thicknesses of the liners, use scissors to repeatedly make snips about 1 1/2 inches in length. Then bend some of the resulting petals forward and "fluff" others to create the dimensional look of a blossom.

Spring

Rainy Day Pictures

Perk up a rainy day with an art project that's a lot of fun. On light gray or blue construction paper, color a rainy day scene—but omit the raindrops. Fill a spray bottle with 1 cup of water and 1/4 cup of nonchlorine bleach. Protect your clothing with a smock before spraying your artwork with the bleach solution. (Cut neck- and armholes in a trash bag for a disposable smock.) Once dry, the droplets will lighten the paper, giving the look of a shower.

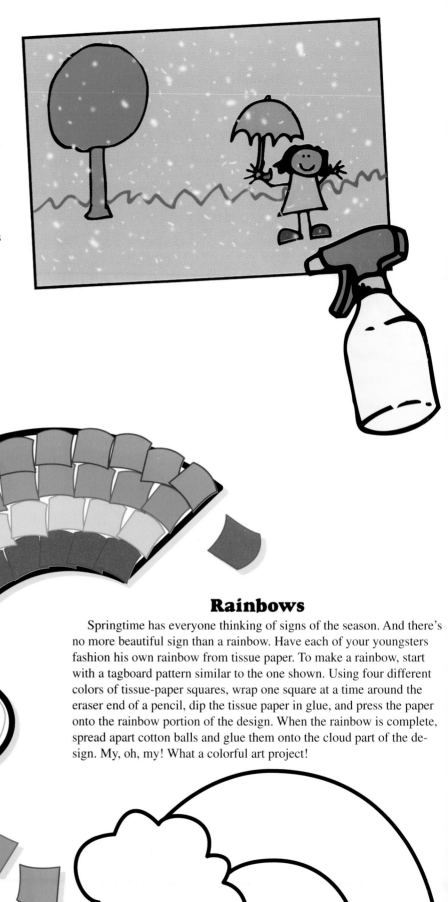

Rainbows

Springtime has everyone thinking of signs of the season. And there's no more beautiful sign than a rainbow. Have each of your youngsters fashion his own rainbow from tissue paper. To make a rainbow, start with a tagboard pattern similar to the one shown. Using four different colors of tissue-paper squares, wrap one square at a time around the eraser end of a pencil, dip the tissue paper in glue, and press the paper onto the rainbow portion of the design. When the rainbow is complete, spread apart cotton balls and glue them onto the cloud part of the design. My, oh, my! What a colorful art project!

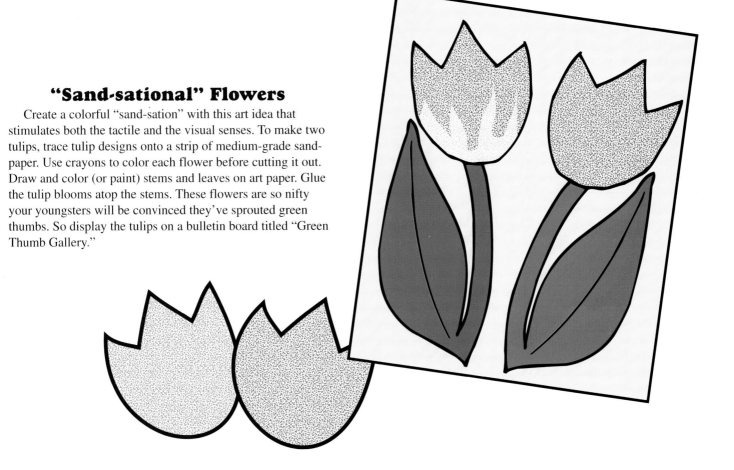

"Sand-sational" Flowers

Create a colorful "sand-sation" with this art idea that stimulates both the tactile and the visual senses. To make two tulips, trace tulip designs onto a strip of medium-grade sandpaper. Use crayons to color each flower before cutting it out. Draw and color (or paint) stems and leaves on art paper. Glue the tulip blooms atop the stems. These flowers are so nifty your youngsters will be convinced they've sprouted green thumbs. So display the tulips on a bulletin board titled "Green Thumb Gallery."

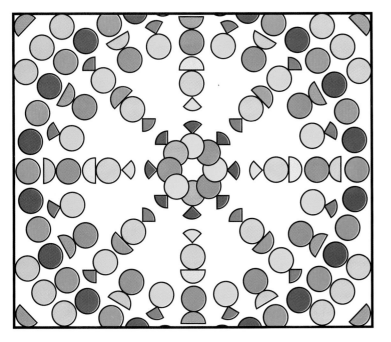

Peel-And-Stick Designs

When the first rainy day of spring arrives, be on the spot with a simple art activity that students will love. Give each child a piece of construction paper and a supply of colorful peel-and-stick dots. Encourage students to use the dots to create one-of-a-kind designs or pictures. Provide scissors and suggest cutting some of the dots in halves or fourths. You're sure to spot some master designers in no time!

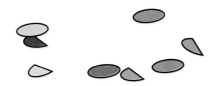

Spring

May Flowers

Fill a spring bulletin board with these three-dimensional blossoms.

Steps:

1. Cut a paper-towel tube into 1/2-inch sections.
2. Pour glue onto a piece of waxed paper.
3. To make the flower petals, dip the edges of each section—one at a time—into the glue. Then place the moistened edges on a piece of tissue paper. Follow the same procedure to make three to four green leaves.
4. Allow to dry; then trim the excess tissue around each section.
5. To make the flower center, roll a 4" x 1/2" strip of tagboard into a tight circle and secure with tape.
6. Glue each petal to the center section and to its neighboring petal.
7. Cut an 8" x 1/2" piece of tagboard to make a stem. Glue the leaves to the stem.
8. Glue the flower to the stem.

Calico Egg Wreaths

Decorate for Eastertime with beautiful calico egg wreaths. Ask your students' parents for donations of a variety of calico fabrics. To make the eggs, provide each student with a small egg pattern and tagboard. Have each student trace his pattern on the tagboard 15 times and then cut out the eggs. Next have students cut pieces of fabric (each large enough to cover an egg pattern). After gluing fabric to each egg, the student trims off the excess for a smooth egg shape. To complete the project, have the student glue the eggs together in a wreath shape. Make bows for the wreaths with oversized yarn.

Spring Abstracts

Give each child a 9" x 12" piece of white paper. Have the student draw a simple spring object on his paper: butterfly, bird, flower, kite and cloud, bunny, etc. Encourage students to make their drawings as large as possible in order to fill the paper. After the drawing is complete, have the child draw a three-inch grid on top of his drawing using a ruler. The student then chooses three to four crayons or markers. Tell students to fill up every enclosed area of their pictures, trying to mix colors up so that they don't have the same color side by side. After coloring, have students outline all lines with a black marker or crayon.

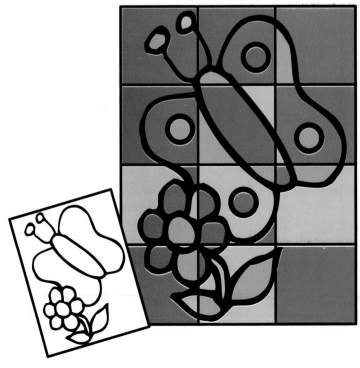

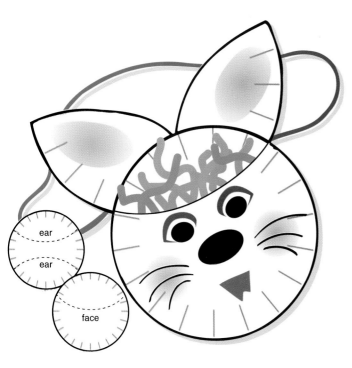

Whiskers And Fur

Tuck a few treats into these student-made baskets to top off your Easter festivities. Begin with three paper plates per basket. To create the ears, draw two curved lines on a plate as shown. Cut on the curves; then discard the middle section. For the bunny's face, draw a single curve (as shown) on another plate. Cut on the curve; then discard the smaller piece. Invert the face piece and glue or staple it atop an uncut paper plate. Glue or staple one end of each ear beneath the uncut plate. Using a makeup brush and blush, apply color to the cheeks and the insides of the ears. Cut out and attach construction-paper features; then draw on whiskers. To complete the project, tuck some cellophane grass into the opening. To create a carrying handle, punch two holes in the uncut plate and thread with yarn. Before long your classroom will be brimming with bunnies!

Springtime Vases

Since imitation is the sincerest form of flattery, Mother Nature should be rather proud of these pussy willow and forsythia impostors. Begin by cutting a vase shape from construction paper, wallpaper, or fabric. Glue the vase cutout near the bottom of a large piece of construction paper. Use brown crayon to draw stems extending upward from the vase. For pussy willows, decorate some stems by gluing on puffed rice cereal. For forsythia, decorate the remaining stems with small pieces of yellow tissue paper. Is that the faint, sweet fragrance of forsythia that I smell, or is it just my imagination?

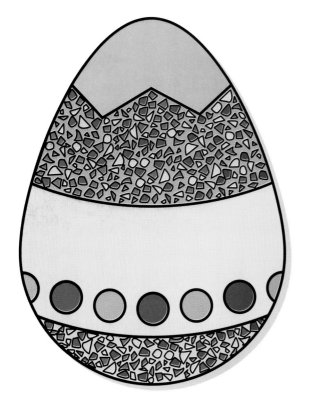

Eggshell Art

Crushed eggshells add interesting texture to any art project, but at Easter they seem "egg-ceptionally" appropriate as an art medium. Ask your students to collect rinsed and dried eggshells for this project. After crushing the eggshells, equally divide them into several containers. Dye the eggshells using water, food coloring, and vinegar. When the desired colors are achieved, drain the containers, and scatter the eggshells on several layers of paper towels to dry.

On poster-board egg cutouts, draw designs. Fill one of the areas with a thick coat of glue. Sprinkle eggshells of your color choice atop this section. Continue gluing and adding eggshells until the desired effect is achieved. Complete the project using Elmer's GluColors™, glitter, sequins, rhinestones, ribbon, or lace as desired.

Spring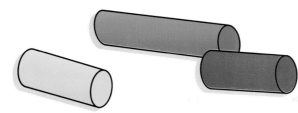

Stained-Glass Easter Eggs

To design these colorful and eye-catching eggs, try this unusual technique. Cut a piece of blank construction paper into an egg shape. Draw lines to divide the egg into small sections. Squeeze white glue along the lines. Outline the egg shape with glue also. Let the glue dry overnight. The lines will dry clear, but can still be seen. Color in each section with colored chalk.

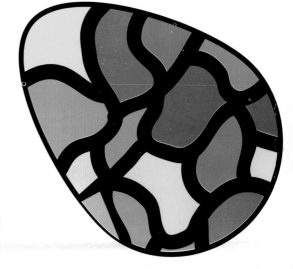

Peekaboo Eggs

These Easter eggs will surprise students. Dip fingertips in watercolor paint and print one sheet of white construction paper with colored dots. Let the paint dry, and cut out a large egg shape. Cut intersecting lines (as shown) in the center of the egg and roll the points back around a pencil. Trace around the egg on another sheet of white construction paper and cut out. Draw and color a scene in the middle of the white egg. Glue the two cutouts together so the scene is displayed through the opening. Students will love peeking inside their eggshells to discover what's inside.

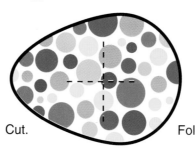

Cut.   Fold back.

Mexican Flowers

These big, bold, tissue-paper flowers make a colorful border for a bulletin board. Students can also make them to give to moms on Mother's Day.

Materials needed for each child:
four 10" squares of tissue paper (of two or more colors)
scissors
stapler

Steps:
1. Place tissue-paper squares together, alternating colors.
2. Fold the squares in half and in half again as shown.
3. Staple the folded corner.
4. Trim the tissue paper, rounding the corners as shown.
5. Gently pull the tissue paper apart to open the flowers.

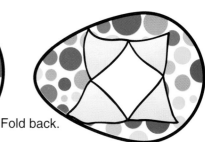

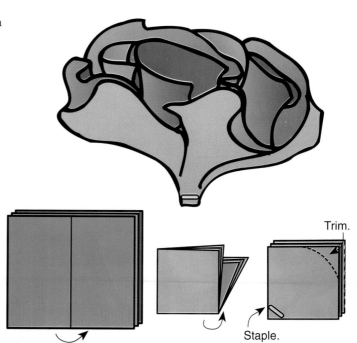

Trim.

Staple.

Bunny Bookmark

With this radiant rabbit bookmark in place, a youngster—or an adult for that matter—will be anxious to hop back between the covers of an unfinished book. To make a bookmark, paint a tongue depressor with white tempera paint. Use a fine-tip black marker to draw a face on the depressor once the paint has dried. For ears, cut a shape similar to the one shown from felt. Using a Q-tip®, apply blusher to what will be the insides of the ears and to the cheek area of the face. Tie a knot in the middle of the felt ears before gluing them to the back of the tongue depressor. If youngsters would like to give these bookmarks as gifts, have each of them write a cheerful greeting or message below the rabbit face on his bookmark.

Ear pattern

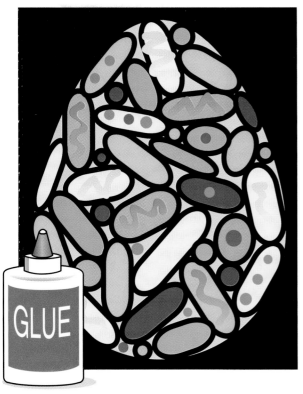

"Egg-ceptional" Eggs

Inspire intricately detailed egg art with this approach. To begin, trace a large egg shape onto art paper. Inside the egg outline, draw abstract designs. Color the designs and cut out the egg shape. Mount the egg onto construction paper. Using black puff paint or tinted glue, trace over the lines drawn previously. Complete the artwork by using other colors of puff paint or glue to add the finishing touches.

Chick Easter Basket

Create a sensation by replacing your usual basket project with this spring chick. Begin by using the patterns on page 104 to make a head cutout, upper and lower beak cutouts, two wing cutouts, two feet cutouts, and two eye cutouts. Attach the eyes to the head. To assemble the beak, begin by cutting along the dotted beak lines and folding along the double lines. Then glue the upper and lower beak to the head. Glue or tape each of the chick's body parts to a 12-ounce plastic bowl. Feathers may be added if desired. Fill the bowl with cellophane grass and treats.

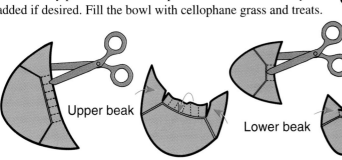

Upper beak

Lower beak

Patterns

Use with "Chick Easter Basket" on page 103.

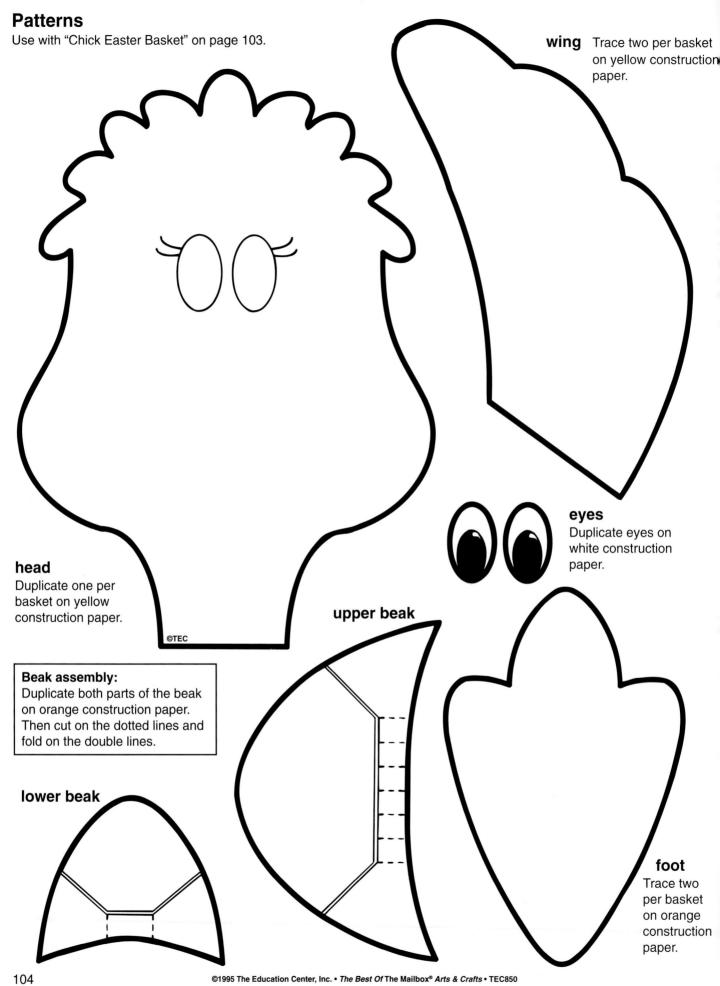

wing Trace two per basket on yellow construction paper.

eyes Duplicate eyes on white construction paper.

head Duplicate one per basket on yellow construction paper.

©TEC

upper beak

Beak assembly: Duplicate both parts of the beak on orange construction paper. Then cut on the dotted lines and fold on the double lines.

lower beak

foot Trace two per basket on orange construction paper.

Boppin' Bunnies

Like Weebles, these bunnies wobble but they don't fall down! Mix plaster of paris according to box directions, and fill the bottom section of a large plastic egg 2/3 full of the mixture. Place the egg on an upside-down egg carton, so that the plaster of paris will dry level. (You may want to do this the day before you intend to decorate your egg.) Glue the top section of the egg to the bottom section. To transform your egg into a bunny, use craft glue to attach felt or construction-paper ears and facial features, as well as a cotton-ball tail. Add finishing touches with a permanent marker. Not only are these bunnies beauteous, but they can also bop with the best of them!

Party Favor Bags

Have your youngsters create their own party bags with sponges, paint, markers, and crayons. To begin decorating a plain white bag, sponge-print it with a chick-, rabbit-, or lamb-shaped sponge and tempera paint. After the paint is dry, use crayons and markers to finish the picture by adding clouds, grass, Easter eggs, and other elements. Roll down the top of the bag and place some cellophane or shredded tissue-paper grass inside. When youngsters need containers for egg hunts or for party favors, they have a great place to put them.

Spring

Fantasy Eggs

The Easter bunny loves to decorate eggs and so will your youngsters! To make one egg, begin with two identical giant eggs cut from bulletin-board paper. Choose from an assortment of craft scraps and supplies to decorate each egg. Eggs may be painted, glittered, colored, or decorated collage style with gift wrap or wallpaper scraps. Place the decorated egg cutouts back-to-back. Staple most of the way around the eggs. Stuff crumpled newspaper into the opening before stapling the eggs closed. Punch a hole in the top of the egg, insert yarn for hanging, and tie the yarn ends. My, oh, my! These eggs are an Easter bunny's fantasy.

Jigsaw Puzzle Pins

What do you get when you recycle an old jigsaw puzzle? A great Mother's Day gift! Place four to six puzzle pieces next to and/or on top of each other; then glue them in place. After the glue has dried, paint the printed surface of the puzzle pieces with fabric paints. Swirl the paints around and use a variety of colors. Let the paints dry for several hours. Glue a pin back (available in craft stores) to the cardboard side of each painted puzzle design. Allow the glue to dry; then get ready to surprise Mom with her unique Mother's Day pin!

Wing It

If you find that your box of construction-paper scraps is becoming a bit too full, it's time to wing it. To make a butterfly from construction-paper scraps, fill a Ziploc® bag with torn or cut scraps. Seal the bag. Tie it with a piece of ribbon or a pipe cleaner. Suspend the butterfly from the ceiling or use it to embellish a bulletin board.

Tulips For Mom

Have your youngsters make colorful floral greetings to surprise and delight their moms on Mother's Day. To make a greeting, trace a symmetrical tulip shape onto 9" x 12" (or larger) wallpaper samples two times and onto colorful, lined paper once. Cut out each tulip shape. After writing and correcting a first draft of your message, use a colorful felt-tip marker to copy it onto the lined paper cutout. Place the message between the tulip-shaped wallpaper covers, punch holes in the left margin, and fasten the sheets together with brads. Attach a 1 1/2" x 12" strip of green construction paper at the lower edge of the inside back cover. Using a contrasting marker, write "Happy Mother's Day!" on the front cover and "Love, [your signature]" on the strip. Fold the strip so that it is concealed between the covers if desired. Happy day, Mom!

Dear Mom,
Thank you for all the nice things you do for me.
I love you.

Love Jay

Hats Off To Mom

Youngsters can tip their hats to their mothers with these cheerful greetings. To make a greeting card, color and cut out a copy of the head and hats on page 109. Fold a sheet of construction paper forward three inches from the bottom. Then staple the folded paper to form a pocket, and store the hat cutouts inside. On the pocket, write "Thanks for the many jobs you do." Glue the mom cutout above the pocket, and glue some lace at the neckline. Use crayons, glue, and construction paper to decorate the head cutout to resemble your mother. Then cut a 3/4" slit where indicated. Fold the upper portion of the construction paper forward, aligning it with the bottom fold. On the outer portion of this flap, write "Hats off to you, Mom!"

Thanks for the many jobs you do.

Andrew

Hats off to you, Mom!

Shy Violets

Set the mood for this activity by displaying several colors of blooming violets. To make a flowerpot, cut a 4 1/2" x 6" sheet of yellow construction paper into a rounded shape. Then cut ovals from 1 1/2"-wide blue, pink, or lavender crepe-paper strips. Also cut several heart-shaped leaves from green construction paper. Glue the yellow pot cutout near the bottom of a sheet of black construction paper. Glue leaf shapes near—but not above—the top of the pot. Then glue the crepe-paper ovals in clusters of five above the pot to resemble violet petals. Glue only near the center of each cluster. Glue a yellow circle cutout (cut from the remaining yellow scraps) in the center of each cluster of ovals. Voilà, a floral masterpiece!

Spring 🌷🌷

Umbrella Weather

When it's raining cats and dogs outside, have youngsters create their own personal downpours. To begin, use a white crayon to draw large raindrops on a 12" x 18" sheet of white art paper. Retrace each raindrop and add a crescent-shaped highlight to each with the white crayon. (Or, for tons of fun, draw tiny dogs and cats falling through the air instead of raindrops.) Then brush a thin wash of dark blue, purple, or black watercolor on the entire page. Set this background page aside to dry. Cut a thin paper plate in half and cut scallops from the straight edge. Paint an original design onto the bottom of the plate, and allow it to dry. Trace your hand and forearm onto tan or brown paper, and cut it out. Then arrange the plate half, the hand/arm cutout, a strip of black construction paper, and a J-shaped cutout on your raindrop background as shown. Fold the finger cutouts over the handle of the umbrella, and glue the pieces in place to complete the rainy-day effect.

Leap Into Spring

Get the hop on springtime art with these paper-plate amphibians. For this project, you will need a thin white paper plate, a pencil, a paintbrush, green tempera paint, a red crayon, scissors, glue, a 3 1/2" x 2" red construction-paper rectangle, two 2" white construction-paper squares, two 1" black construction-paper squares, and four 6 1/2" x 3 1/2" green construction-paper rectangles.

To make a frog, fold a paper plate in half and color one inner half red. Then paint the outer surface of the plate green. Allow for drying time. From the red paper rectangle, cut a tongue. From the white and black paper, create eyes. From the green paper cut "arms" and "legs." Glue the eyes, tongue, arms, and legs in place as shown. Look out, Kermit; more great "hoppers" are on the way!

Fantasy Flowers

Create a sensation by converting your classroom into an oversize, student-made flower garden! To make a flower, accordion-fold each of six 9" x 12" sheets of colored construction paper so that the pattern on page 109 fits atop it as shown. Trace the pattern onto each piece of folded paper, cutting on the solid lines. Punch a hole about 1/4" from the short, straight edge of each folded piece. With the folded pieces stacked, thread a 4" length of pipe cleaner through the holes and twist the ends to create a ring. Staple each folded sheet to the adjacent one(s). Gently pull the upper and lower paper edges around to meet, and staple them in place. Attach green tagboard or crepe-paper stem and leaf cutouts to the flower, before suspending it from the ceiling.

Fold.

Use the head and hat patterns with "Hats Off To Mom" on page 107.

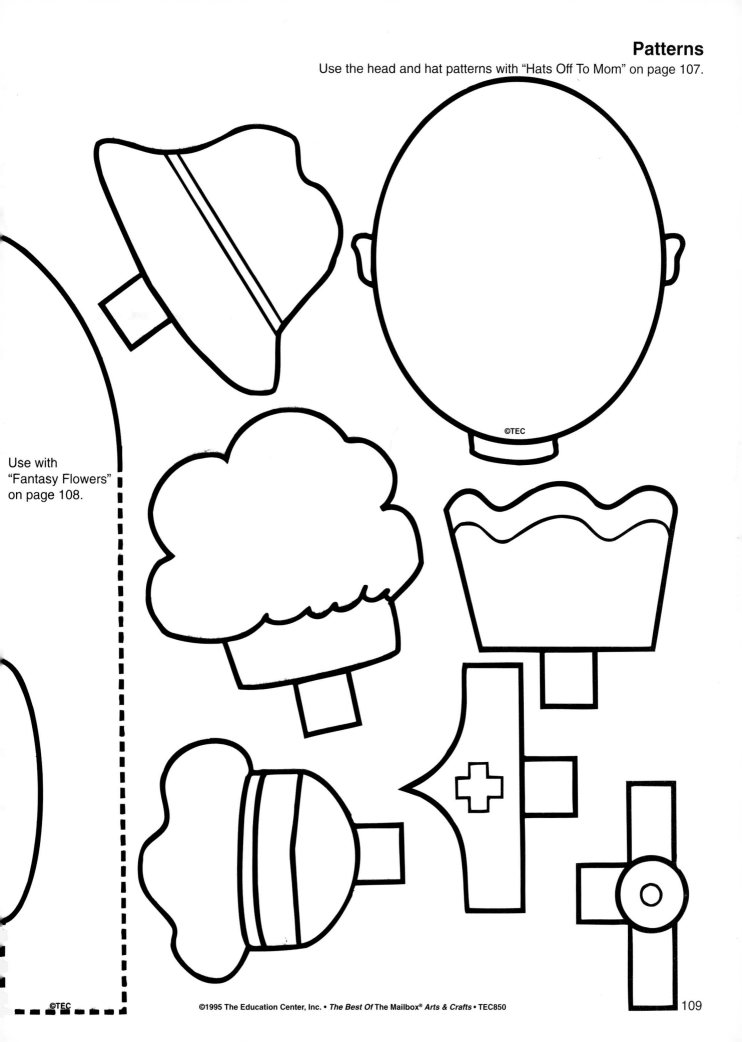

Use with
"Fantasy Flowers"
on page 108.

©TEC

Spring 🌷🌷

Mother's Day Minibooklets

Delight Mom with a tiny booklet honoring her on her special day.

Steps for making one booklet:

1. Fold and/or twist an absorbent paper towel as desired.
2. Dip several portions of the towel into first one, and then another, color of slightly diluted food coloring. Squeeze to remove excess water, unfold the towel, and allow to dry.
3. Cut two 3" x 3" pieces of cardboard.
4. Use glue to cover each piece of cardboard with the dyed paper towel. These are the booklet's covers.
5. Cut an 18" x 2 1/2" strip of construction paper.
6. Accordion-fold the strip into equal-sized sections.
7. Glue one end pleat to the inside front cover and one to the inside back cover.
8. Fill your pages with a Mother's Day poem, a letter to Mom, a story, or anything you like that says, "Thanks, Mom!"

Best Wishes, Mom!

Send Mom a card that celebrates nature as well as her shining qualities! Have students collect small flowers, leaves, and fine grasses. Dry them between newspapers under a stack of heavy books. Drying should take two weeks if plants are small.

Give each student a piece of white paper. Have the student fold his paper in half, then cut a piece of clear Con-Tact® covering slightly bigger than the unfolded paper. After removing the backing from half of the covering, the student attaches it to the back half of the notepaper. Next the child arranges his dried plants on the front of the card. Holding the plants down, he gradually peels off the rest of the backing and smooths the covering over the arrangement. Instruct students to trim the edges before filling their cards with special messages for Mom.

Mother's Day Hat Magnets

With just a few simple materials and lots of your loving patience, students can make beautiful refrigerator magnets for their moms.

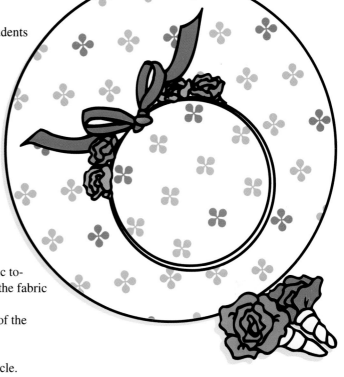

Materials needed for one hat:

scissors
3" tagboard circle
enough fabric to make three 3"
  circles (Use fabric that has small
  patterns.)
14" piece of narrow, coordinating
  ribbon

pop bottle cap
craft glue
needle and thread
1" strip of magnetic tape
small silk or fabric
  flowers, bows, ribbons,
  netting, etc.

Steps:

1. Cut three 3-inch circles from the fabric. (Hint: Trace the tagboard circle.)
2. Cover the bottle cap with one of the fabric circles. Gather the fabric together inside the bottle cap; then use the needle and thread to sew the fabric together.
3. Lightly glue the other two fabric circles to the top and the bottom of the tagboard circle.
4. Glue the magnetic strip in the middle of the fabric-covered circle.
5. Glue the covered bottle cap to the opposite side of the tagboard circle. Place the cap a little off-center, toward the back of the circle.
6. Tie the ribbon around the covered bottle cap.
7. Decorate the hat with small silk flowers, bows, ribbons, netting, etc.

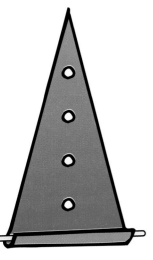

Paper Beads

Turn unused wrapping paper and wallpaper into easy-to-make decorative beads for Mother's Day. Have students cut long triangle shapes from the paper. Each triangle should have a base of about 3/4 inches and a height of 5 1/2 inches. With the blank side up, have the student dot glue down the middle of each triangle. He then places a round toothpick at the large end of the triangle and rolls up the paper to form a bead. After removing the toothpicks, allow the beads to dry. After drying, the beads look like painted wooden or ceramic ones. Use fishing line or craft wire to string the beads into bracelets and necklaces.

Spring

Say It With A Card

Handmade cards are always a hit with moms on Mother's Day. Make yours extraspecial with fabric and yarn scraps. Spray-starch scrap fabric to make it easier for students to cut out shapes without fraying. Have students glue their fabric cutouts to folded pieces of construction paper and add accents of yarn.

Miniature Wreath Magnets

Mom will love this attractive country wreath magnet. Cut poster board into small wreath shapes. Glue tiny dried flowers, pinecones, and other decorations onto the wreaths. After drying, add yarn or cloth bows. Attach a piece of magnetic tape to the back of each wreath; then get ready to say, "Happy Mother's Day, Mom!"

"You Really Bowl Me Over, Mom!"

Here's an unusual Mother's Day gift that students will love to make. Cover a kitchen bowl of any size with aluminum foil. Apply three layers of newspaper strips dipped in wallpaper paste over the foil. After drying, remove from the bowl. Gently pull away the foil lining; then paint the bowl with colorful tempera colors. Add a finishing coat of shellac. These bowls are great for serving popcorn or other lightweight snacks. Pass the popcorn, Mom!

Mother's Day Paperweights

Children will be proud to present these unique gifts to mothers. Collect plastic salad dressing bottles. Wash them well. Put plastic flowers inside a bottle; then fill the bottle with colored water. Add a few drops of super-type glue inside the lid before sealing to secure the top. Each paperweight is a unique gift, depending on the size and shape of the bottle and the color the child chooses. The paperweight also makes an attractive window decoration.

I Love You, Mother!

To encourage appreciation for mothers, read the book, *When I Was Young In The Mountains* by Cynthia Ryland. Then let each child make a booklet entitled "I Love You, Mother." Each page begins with "I love you, Mother…." The child completes the sentence and illustrates the page. Staple the pages together with a construction-paper cover. Mothers will be pleased to receive these booklets on Mother's Day.

I Love You, Mother

because you taught me to ride my bike.

I Love You, Mother!

Soap Balls

These fragrant soap balls are nice gifts and are great fun for kids to make. This recipe makes about five, two-inch balls.

Ingredients:
2 cups Ivory Snow® Soap Flakes
1/4 c. water
food coloring
fragrance or flavor extract

Steps:
Mix all other ingredients in a large bowl before adding soap flakes. The mixture will look crumbly. Shape into balls, packing firmly. Smooth gently. Let the soap balls dry. Wrap each ball in a square of netting and tie with a ribbon bow.

Spring

Take Note

Your youngsters can fashion these note holders to give to their mothers on Mother's Day. To make the back of the note holder, position one craft stick horizontally on a sheet of waxed paper. Above the stick, place ten more. Press all 11 sticks together. Along each side, run a trail of glue. While the glue is drying, create and glue a similar configuration of seven sticks (front of the note holder) and another of two sticks (bottom of the note holder). For each of the two sides of the note holder, glue eight sticks one atop the other. When all of these sections have dried, glue them together. (Use rubber bands to hold the pieces in place until the glue dries.) For a hanger, glue two sticks to the back of the note holder and to each other in an inverted *v* shape. When the glue is dry, decorate the note holder with a photograph, fabric notions, flowers, or other miscellaneous craft supplies. Complete the project by slipping a stack of 3 1/4" x 4" notes in the holder.

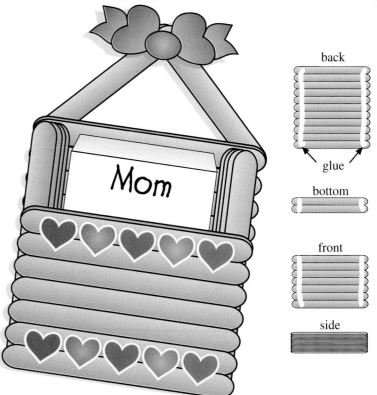

Sweets For The Sweet

What a sweet way to treat Mom on Mother's Day! To make this Mother's Day greeting card, fold a sheet of 12" x 18" art paper twice to create a 3/4" spine. Decorate the front of the card with flowery art. Write "A big bunch of kisses just for you! Love, [your name]" on the inside left side of the card. Around this writing, draw additional flowers. Next decorate the inside right side of the card with four candy-kiss flowers.

To make a candy-kiss flower, begin with two 3 1/2" squares of construction paper. Cut each square as shown to create flower petals. Then cut a 3 1/2" x 1 1/2" green piece of construction paper to make a leaf. Glue the leaf, then the two petal pieces, to the card. Glue on a foil-wrapped candy kiss for the flower center. Repeat this process to create three additional flowers.

Perky Posies

If your youngsters gather the flowers for this project in April, the flowers will be ready to become part of a masterpiece in May. To make a pressed flower bouquet, choose and locate several delicate flowers. Flowers like primrose, bluebonnet, and black-eyed Susan are especially good choices for this project. Press the flowers between the pages of weighted catalogs. Several weeks later, glue a few of the dried, pressed flowers to a mat board or a piece of construction paper or tagboard. When the glue is dry, laminate the project. Display each project on a tagboard easel for easy viewing. (See the diagrams for an easy-to-make easel.)

Sweet Surprise

Moms will appreciate these aromatic kitchen ornaments and students will be delighted to have made them. Mix two cups of applesauce with ground cinnamon (about 12 ounces) to form a dough. Roll out the dough, cut it with cookie cutters, and make a hole in the top of each cutout. Dry the cutouts atop a rack, and insert string or ribbon in the holes for hanging. Decorate as desired. Recommend that moms hang these ornaments where steam will caress them, releasing their spicy scent.

Colossal Mother's Day Flowers

Here's a tribute that mothers can really appreciate. To make a colossal flower, draw a picture of your mother or other female caretaker on a large circle of construction paper. Then cut out a giant six-petal flower design with a center the size of the portrait. Glue the portrait to the flower cutout. Label the flower so others will be able to identify the face. Then attach the flower to the display surface so that only the center and the tips of the petals touch the surface, creating a three-dimensional effect. With the eye-appealing combination of colossal-size flowers and three-dimensional mounting, passersby are going to be stopping by to take a closer look. Invite moms and other female caretakers in for refreshments and to see their youngsters' artwork.

Spring 🌷🌷

Spring Bluebonnets

Share Tomie dePaola's wonderful story *The Legend Of The Bluebonnet* as your students create their own bluebonnet bouquets.

Materials for one bluebonnet:
wooden shish kebab skewer
two plastic six-pack rings
scissors
blue and white spray paint

Steps:

1. Cut the two six-pack rings into 12 oval-shaped rings.
2. Fold an oval ring upward, making sure that the ends are atop each other.
3. Holding the folded ends together, carefully push them onto the pointed end of the wooden skewer. Push the ring about three-fourths of the way down the skewer.
4. Repeat Steps 2 and 3, alternately turning the rings to hide the skewer and create the look of blossoms.
5. Use about 12 rings to make one flower. Fold the last ring over the point of the skewer to form the end of the blossom.
6. Spray the bottom three-fourths of the rings with blue paint. Add white paint to the top of the flower. The paints will splatter and mix, enhancing the appearance of the final product.

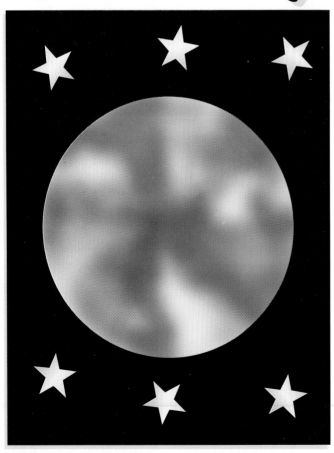

We Love Our Earth!

Earth Day, every day! Honor Mother Earth on April 22 with a unique two-in-one project.

Materials for each student:
one paper coffee filter
one 9" x 12" sheet of white art paper
one 9" x 12" sheet of black construction paper
yellow, blue, green, and purple watercolors
Q-tips®
scissors
glue
silver or gold gummed stars
water

Steps:

1. Wet a paper coffee filter.
2. Place the filter on the white art paper.
3. Use Q-tips® to dab yellow, blue, green, and purple watercolors onto the filter. Cover the entire filter with color. Add more water to the filter if it dries too quickly.
4. Allow the filter to dry.
5. Remove the filter. A beautiful earth shape will be left on the art paper.
6. Cut out the earth shape and glue it onto the black construction paper.
7. Add silver or gold gummed stars around the earth.

Don't throw away those painted coffee filters—turn them into butterflies! Fold a filter in half. Then gather it in the middle and tie it off with a pipe cleaner. Two art projects in one!

Father's Day Key Chain

Say Happy Father's Day with a creative clay key chain! Using the clay recipe below, have each child make a pottery bead. The bead may be any shape. Be sure that a large hole (about the size of a pencil) is in the center of the bead. Allow the beads to dry before painting; then seal with an acrylic spray. After drying (which will take approximately one to two days), string a piece of suede, jute, or leather through the hole. Keys may then be placed on the "string" before tying. Or inexpensive key rings can be purchased to hold the keys.

Play Clay

Ingredients: 1 cup cornstarch, 2 cups (1 lb.) baking soda, 1 1/2 cups cold water

Procedure: Combine ingredients in saucepan. Stir until smooth. Cook over medium heat until mix reaches consistency of slightly dry mashed potatoes. When mixture forms a ball, turn onto plate and cover with a damp cloth. When cool, knead until pliable. May be stored in plastic bag in refrigerator for up to two weeks.

Dad's Wallet

Surprise Dad with a wallet full of special coupons. Each child will need a 12" x 18" piece of gift wrap (or colored construction paper).

Steps:
1. With the plain side up, fold the paper in half lengthwise and crosswise; then unfold.
2. Fold all four corners to the center fold line.
3. Fold the tips of the triangles as illustrated.
4. Fold top and bottom to the middle.
5. Now turn the wallet over.
6. Fold each side to the middle.
7. Fold along the dotted line.

Now have students write coupons, redeemable at any time, that they can place in the wallets for their dads. Some suggestions include washing the car, cleaning out the garage, taking out the garbage, breakfast in bed, etc.

Father's Day Nature Collage

Dads will be proud to hang these "earthy" works of art! Have each child bring in a section of old, weathered board or a piece of bark. Gather assorted materials from outdoors that can be used to make nature collages, such as colorful stones and pebbles, twigs, acorns, leaves, nuts, and dried flowers. Arrange them on the board and attach with glue. Preserve with acrylic spray if desired. Drill two holes at the top of the board and thread with twine for hanging.

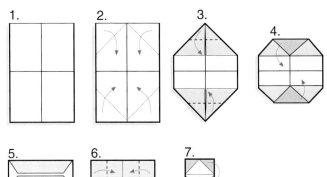

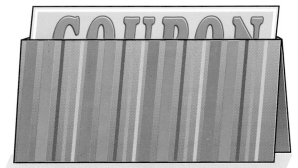

Decorative Paper Bags

Follow this step-by-step plan to create a decorative paper bag. Use the bag to hold a Father's Day gift, or at any other time of the year. After learning these steps, students can experiment with other sizes and types of paper. To begin, each child needs a 12" x 18" sheet of light-colored construction paper.

Steps:

1. Use a ruler and lightly draw all the lines shown. The parts marked **a** are the sides of the bag and are the same size. The parts marked **b** are the front and back of the bag, and are also the same size. The pieces marked **c** make up the bottom of the bag.
2. Cut out the corners as shown.
3. Use a ruler and scissors to score all the lines as follows: place the ruler beside a line; then trace along the line with scissors to create a light crease.
4. Fold over the top flap and glue down. This creates a strong edge that prevents the bag from tearing easily.

5. Turn the paper over to decorate. Use crayons, markers, paints, and glitter to personalize the front and back sections of the bag.
6. Next fold the bag at all vertical creases; then glue together at the flap.
7. Fold the bottom flaps under and glue. Fold the short flaps first, then the longer flaps.
8. Gently push in the sides along the scored lines.
9. Pinch shut the top of the bag and punch two holes through the front and back sections.
10. To make handles, thread ribbon or yarn through the holes on the front of the bag. Tie the ends of the yarn in knots on the inside of the bag. Do the same for the back of the bag.

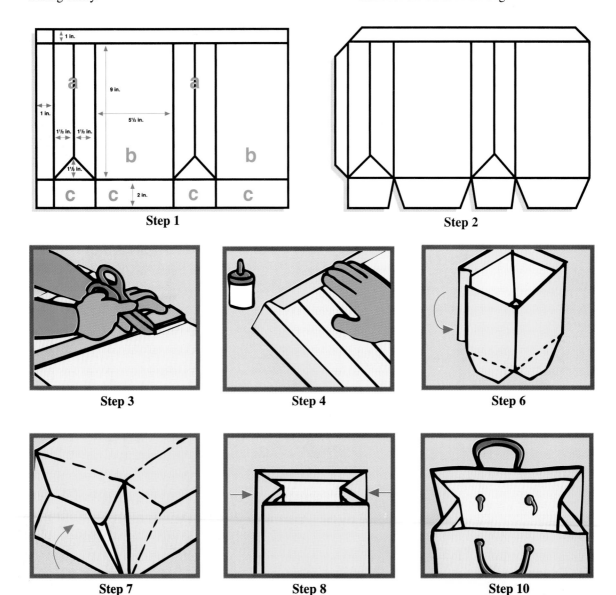

Just For Dad!

Strengthen family ties with these colorful cards! To make this unique Father's Day greeting, fold a 4" x 18" strip of construction paper in half; then trace the tie pattern (page 96) onto the folded paper. Cut on the resulting outlines—not on the fold. Next trace the tie pattern onto colorful lined paper. (Do not fold the lined paper.) Cut approximately 1/8 inch inside the resulting outline. After writing and correcting a first draft of a personalized Father's Day message, use a colorful felt-tip marker to copy it onto the lined paper cutout. Glue this message inside the folded tie cutout. Using crayons or markers, decorate the front cover of the resulting card. Happy Father's Day!

I'm so glad there are family "ties" between us! Happy Father's Day!

Love, EllieAnna

Especially For Dad

Dads will treasure these Father's Day greetings for years to come. Onto the lower halves of sheets of construction paper, duplicate the saying, "Anyone can be a father, but it takes someone special to be a daddy." To make a Father's Day greeting, press paint-covered hands in the upper corners of one copy. Allow the handprints to dry. Then glue—between the handprints—a photo that has been trimmed into a heart shape. Mount the construction paper on a larger sheet of colored tagboard. Finish this sentiment by gluing pasta (tinted or plain) around the tagboard frame.

Anyone can be a father, but it takes someone special to be a daddy.

Spring 🌷🌷

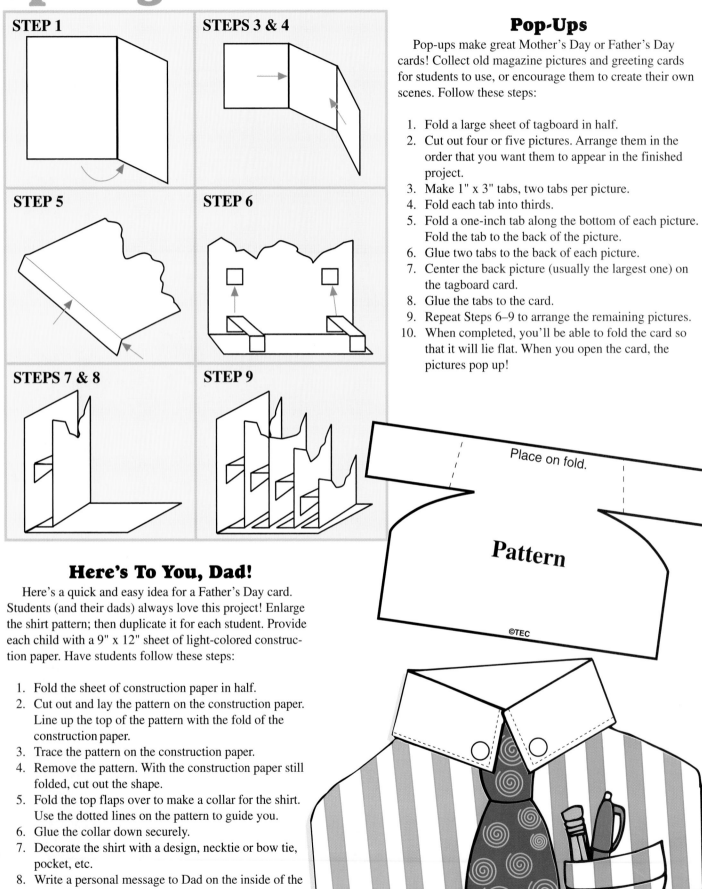

STEP 1

STEPS 3 & 4

STEP 5

STEP 6

STEPS 7 & 8

STEP 9

Pop-Ups

Pop-ups make great Mother's Day or Father's Day cards! Collect old magazine pictures and greeting cards for students to use, or encourage them to create their own scenes. Follow these steps:

1. Fold a large sheet of tagboard in half.
2. Cut out four or five pictures. Arrange them in the order that you want them to appear in the finished project.
3. Make 1" x 3" tabs, two tabs per picture.
4. Fold each tab into thirds.
5. Fold a one-inch tab along the bottom of each picture. Fold the tab to the back of the picture.
6. Glue two tabs to the back of each picture.
7. Center the back picture (usually the largest one) on the tagboard card.
8. Glue the tabs to the card.
9. Repeat Steps 6–9 to arrange the remaining pictures.
10. When completed, you'll be able to fold the card so that it will lie flat. When you open the card, the pictures pop up!

Place on fold.

Pattern

©TEC

Here's To You, Dad!

Here's a quick and easy idea for a Father's Day card. Students (and their dads) always love this project! Enlarge the shirt pattern; then duplicate it for each student. Provide each child with a 9" x 12" sheet of light-colored construction paper. Have students follow these steps:

1. Fold the sheet of construction paper in half.
2. Cut out and lay the pattern on the construction paper. Line up the top of the pattern with the fold of the construction paper.
3. Trace the pattern on the construction paper.
4. Remove the pattern. With the construction paper still folded, cut out the shape.
5. Fold the top flaps over to make a collar for the shirt. Use the dotted lines on the pattern to guide you.
6. Glue the collar down securely.
7. Decorate the shirt with a design, necktie or bow tie, pocket, etc.
8. Write a personal message to Dad on the inside of the card.

Mouthwatering Melons

This easy-to-achieve, sponge-printed effect is created with markers and tissues. Cut tagboard to resemble a watermelon slice. Fold a tissue repeatedly until it's about the size of a quarter. Color one side of the tissue with a dark green marker; then repeatedly press the colored tissue near the rounded edge of the tagboard. Using another folded tissue and a light green marker, add a lighter strip of green tissue imprints adjacent to the dark green ones. Use a third folded tissue and a red marker to press color onto the remainder of the tagboard cutout. Glue on or draw watermelon seeds.

Really tempt your taste buds by working your way through the melon world with this technique. Hmmmm! Should we make the honeydews or the cantaloupes next?

The Deep Blue Sea

Youngsters will be entranced by the sparkling blue "ocean" waters in these tiny kid-made aquariums. To make an aquarium, decorate the outside of a clean, empty baby food jar with fish stickers. Put a few small shells inside. Nearly fill the jar with water. To the water, add a drop or two of food coloring and some blue glitter. Use a hot glue gun to seal the lid of each youngster's jar to prevent leaking. Who could resist shaking these miniaquariums to watch the fishes' glittering ocean backdrop?

Spring 🌷🌷

Marvelous Monarchs

Attract lots of attention with a display of these fancy flyers! To begin, tear orange and yellow tissue paper into small squares. Then, using diluted glue and a paintbrush, cover a 12" x 18" sheet of white construction paper with overlapping tissue-paper squares. Set this project aside to dry. Fold a 12" x 18" sheet of black construction paper in half; then trace the pattern on page 123 onto the folded paper. Cut on the resulting outlines—not on the fold. Unfold the cutout to reveal a butterfly shape. Then, using the illustration (or the pattern on page 123) as a guide, cut an inset for each wing section from the tissue-paper project. Use a black marker to add details to the insets; then glue them atop the wings. Add facial features and details on the outer edges of the wings with a white crayon. Attach bent pipe-cleaner antennae and your project is complete.

Fishy Fanfare

Decorate your room with a school of colorful fish. Trim half of a paper plate as shown; then invert it atop a regular-size paper plate. Align the outer edges, and staple or tape the two plates together to form the fish's body and gill. Cut a supply of one-inch squares from colorful tissue paper. Using diluted glue and a paintbrush, cover the body and gill with overlapping tissue-paper squares. Allow time for the project to dry. Then cut two seven-inch squares from tissue paper. Gather one end of each square. Tape the gathered end of one square to the back of the fish body for a tail. Tape the gathered end of the remaining square beneath the gill for a fin. Add an eye, a mouth, and other details to the fish using construction-paper scraps. What a catch!

Bookmark Mosaics

These bookmarks are a fun way to encourage summer reading. To begin making a bookmark, use a hole puncher and scissors to punch and cut a variety of small shapes from different colors of tissue or construction paper. Set these shapes aside. Then cut two 6" x 3" rectangles from clear Con-Tact® paper. Peel the backing from one rectangle and position the rectangle with the adhesive facing up. Place the cut-out shapes atop the adhesive surface in a desired arrangement. Peel the backing from the remaining rectangle; then place this rectangle (adhesive facedown) atop the cutout arrangement. Trim the edges of the project to create a desired shape. To complete the bookmark, punch a hole in the top of the cutout; then tie a loop of yarn through the hole.

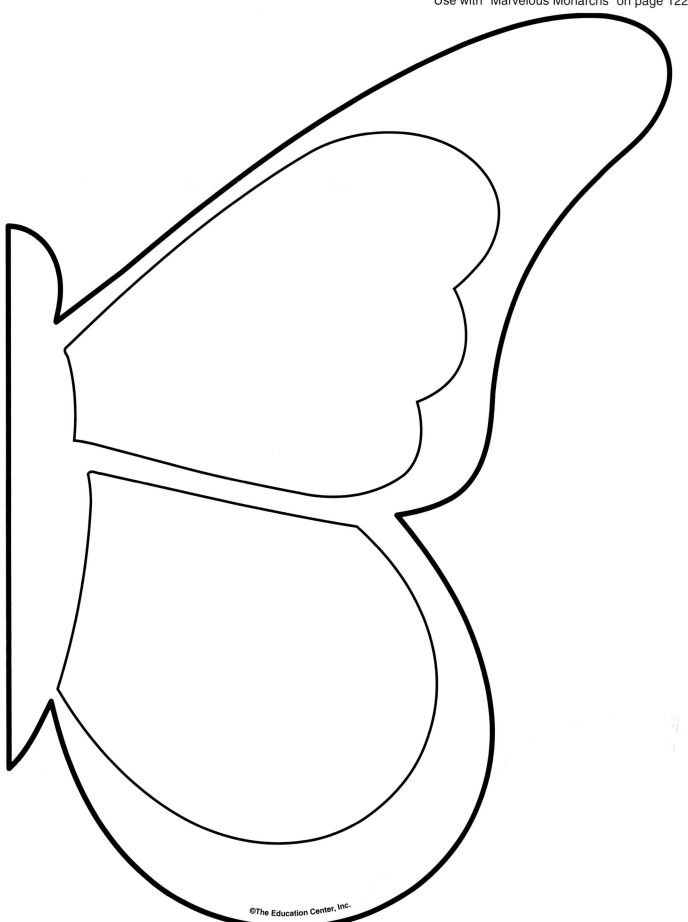

Spring

Visions Of Summertime

Take a sneak peek at summer with a pair of these summery spectacles. To make a pair of spectacles, cut out a construction-paper copy of the patterns on page 125. Then, using construction-paper scraps, crayons, markers, and other desired supplies, glue an assortment of summertime decorations to the front panel of the eyeglasses. To attach each sidepiece, fold on the dotted line and glue the piece to the front panel as shown. For a fun follow-up activity, have youngsters slip on their decorated spectacles and write about their summertime visions. I'm going to Hawaii!

Patriotic Flags

Wave these festive flags during your patriotic celebrations! To make a flag, attach one blue and one white construction-paper star to a red paper-plate half. (See the star patterns on page 125.) Next glue one red, one white, and one blue crepe-paper streamer (each approximately two feet long) beneath and near the center of the paper-plate rim. For a handle, glue one end of a craft stick to the back of the project as shown. Hooray for red, white, and blue!

smart

ong

nice

funny

Daddy,
There is
no tie.
You are
the
BEST
in the world!

Love, Zeb

Family Ties

Father's Day flattery is on its way with these one-of-a-kind greetings! Begin by cutting a tie-shaped tracer from a 4 1/2" x 12" strip of tagboard. Trace this pattern onto a 4 1/2" x 12" strip of construction paper; then use crayons or markers to decorate the resulting shape. Cut out the tie shape. Then fold a 9" x 12" sheet of construction paper in half and glue the cutout to the front. Inside, use a marker to write a personalized message such as the one shown. Happy Father's Day!

124

Use eyeglass patterns with "Visions Of Summertime" on page 124.

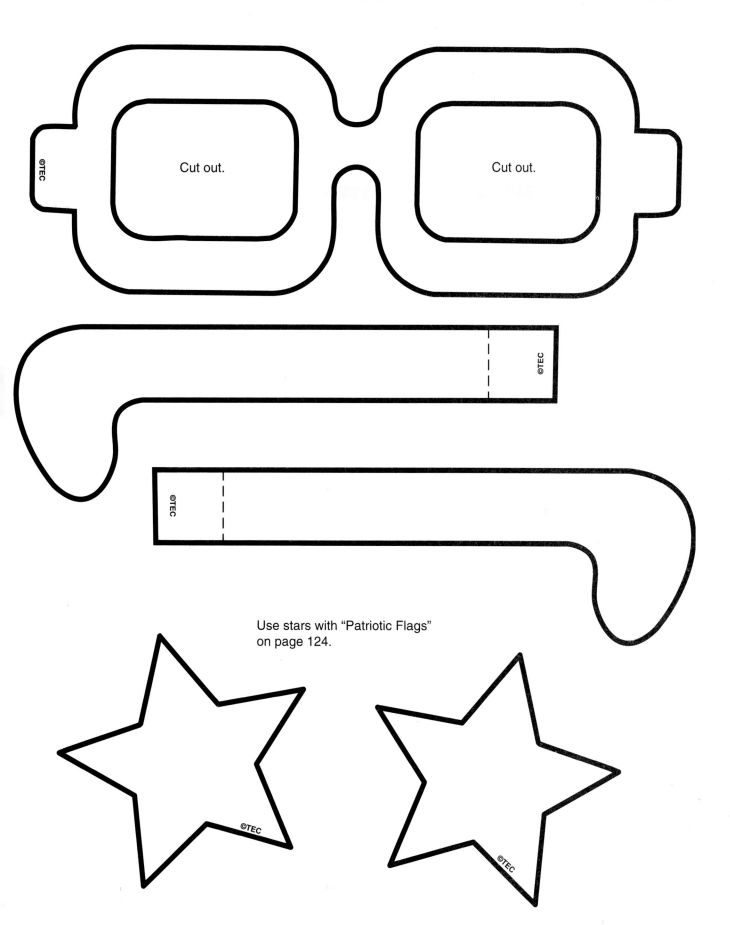

Cut out.

Cut out.

©TEC

©TEC

©TEC

Use stars with "Patriotic Flags"
on page 124.

©TEC

©TEC

Spring

Woven Flags

Here's a patriotic activity that shows the students' support for the United States and Flag Day. Intermediate students can make patriotic flag weavings as part of the special day.

Steps:

1. Glue a 4 1/2" blue square in the upper left corner of a 9" x 12" piece of white construction paper.
2. Cut five or six wavy, horizontal slits in the white paper.
3. Weave one-inch-wide strips of red construction paper in varying lengths through the slits.
4. Attach gold, self-sticking stars to the blue field.
5. Glue a white cut-out star to the tip of each red stripe.

Spring Daydreams

When spring is in the air, it's likely that young minds are starting to wander. Take advantage of that phenomenon with this delightfully fun art project. Divide students into pairs. Place a filmstrip projector in front of an empty wall space. Tape a large piece of white art paper on the wall. With the projector turned on, have one child stand between the light and the wall so that the light causes a shadow of his profile to fall on the white paper. Have the child's partner trace his silhouette lightly with a pencil on the white paper. Remove the paper from the wall. Have the student trace his profile with marker, cut it out, and glue it to a large piece of construction paper. Inside the silhouetted head, have the student draw and color pictures representing some of his favorite daydreams. Post the finished projects on a bulletin board entitled "What A Day For A Daydream!"

Smudge Prints

Try this new trick with old crayons, a perfect time-filler during the last few days of school.

Steps:

1. Sketch and cut out several different sizes and shapes of silhouettes from sturdy paper or tagboard. Houses, trees, cars, pets, and toys are easy. Remember: silhouettes only; no other details are needed.
2. Color the border of each silhouette stencil, covering it darkly. Use a different color on each stencil.
3. Place a stencil on white paper.
4. Holding the stencil firmly with one hand, use the eraser end of a pencil to smudge the crayon onto the white paper. Do this around the entire border of the stencil.
5. When you lift the stencil, you'll see its fuzzy shape outlined on the paper.
6. Use other stencils to create a scene on your paper. For an interesting effect, overlap the stencils when making smudges. Also try coloring the border of a stencil with more than one color. Hint: Rub the eraser on a piece of scratch paper to remove the crayon.

Puzzle Designs

Picture a puzzle with the pieces not quite fitting together, and you've got the idea of this easy technique. First have each student cut a simple silhouette from a sheet of construction paper. He then cuts the silhouette into pieces, placing them on his desk in the correct order. The student then reassembles the pieces on a contrasting color of paper, forming the same basic shape as the original silhouette. The pieces are glued to the paper, leaving a space between each piece.

This technique is both simple and attractive—the perfect project for those days near the end of the school year!

Spring

It's A Grand Ole Flag!

Create a Memorial Day display that pays tribute to Americans who gave their lives for our country. Have students use construction-paper strips to make red, white, and blue paper chains.

- seven blue chains with four links each
- four red chains with six links each
- three white chains with six links each
- three white chains with ten links each
- three red chains with ten links each

Mount the chains on a bulletin board or wall as shown. Have students cut out and attach 50 white paper stars to finish off Old Glory!

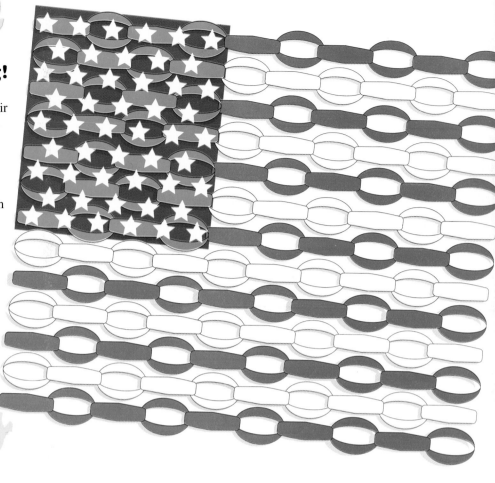

Flowering Raindrops

Capture the beauty of spring flowers in colorful raindrops. Cut two large identical raindrops from waxed paper. Arrange tissue-paper blooms and leaves on one of the raindrops, attaching with tiny bits of paste until the design is complete. Place the second raindrop over the first, sandwiching the flowers between the raindrops. Press with an iron set at a low temperature. Hang the completed raindrops in windows or from the ceiling.

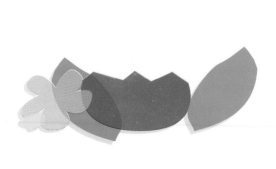

Root Beer Floats

These mouthwatering masterpieces have taste appeal! For each float, draw the outline of a large root beer mug on a 9" x 12" sheet of white construction paper. Squeeze heavy trails of white glue to indicate details on the mug. Also squeeze a heavy trail of glue along the outline. Allow the glue to dry thoroughly. Next brush a coat of brown watercolor paint atop the picture. When the project is dry, cut around the mug shape. Glue the resulting cutout on a 12" x 18" sheet of colorful construction paper. Using white tempera paint, sponge-print a partial scoop of vanilla ice cream protruding from the top of the mug. Attach a touch of cotton froth overflowing from the mug, if desired. To complete the project, trim and glue a colorful, flexible straw jutting from the mug's top. Top off the activity with the *real thing*—root beer floats, that is!

A Fishy Footprint

Get right to the point with this fishy art project! Place several colors of tempera paint in individual containers. Trace the outline of your shoe onto white construction paper. Dip one end of a Q-tip® into one color of paint. Blot the Q-tip on a paper towel to remove excess paint; then paint dots inside your shoe outline. Paint the dots close together so just a small amount of white shows between each dot. Use a different Q-tip for each color of paint. When dry, cut out and mount the shoe shape on a 12" x 18" sheet of light blue construction paper. Add construction-paper fins and tail. Use markers, crayons, or construction-paper scraps to add details and create a habitat for your fish.

Anytime ✂️

Foil Collage

For lots of razzle-dazzle, get creative with food coloring, glue, and foil. To make this project, crumple a piece of aluminum foil; then flatten it, leaving it somewhat crinkled. Add a few drops of food coloring to each of several small containers of white glue. Brush a thin, even coat of several colors of tinted glue onto the foil, occasionally allowing the colors to mix. Allow the glue to dry overnight. Cut the foil into small bits and separate the bits by color. Glue the bits to a black construction-paper background in a collage of a distinctive shape. How's that for sparkle?

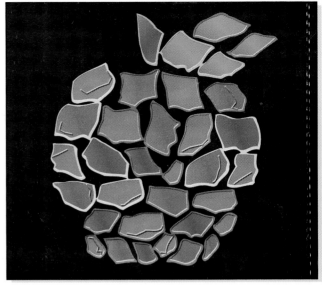

Loopy The Lion

Here's an art project worth roaring about. On yellow construction paper, duplicate the lion pattern (page 131). To make a lion, cut out the pattern and glue on wrinkled brown paper strips for whiskers. Bend the ears forward where they connect to the head. For the lion's mane, you will need a dozen 1 1/4" x 8 1/2" orange paper strips. Glue together the ends of each strip without creasing the strip. To complete the project, glue the strips' ends to the back of the lion's head. This project is a great follow-up activity for any lion-related book.

Patchwork Elephant

Now who could forget seeing a patchwork elephant? Not many people! To begin, fold and crease a sheet of construction paper four times. Unfold the paper and confirm that the folds created 16 nearly equal sections. Draw lines as indicated in the diagram; then cut on the lines for an elephant shape. Decorate each of the remaining areas (sectioned off by fold lines) differently. Trim the rectangular scrap to make the elephant's ear, and decorate it before gluing it in place. Glue on a gray paper tail. Use a marker to add an eye, and tie some yarn around the elephant's trunk. When displayed prominently at home, these elephants may serve as gentle reminders to students about homework assignments. Don't forget! There's a little homework to do.

©The Education Center, Inc.

Anytime ✂

Tropical Treasures

Set the mood for making these pineapple projects by playing hula music as your students work. To make a pineapple, trace the half-oval pattern (page 133) onto a folded sheet of brown construction paper and the jagged pattern (page 133) onto a folded sheet of green construction paper. Cut on the resulting outlines—but not on the folds; then unfold the papers. At about a 20° angle to the fold line, draw a line which extends from one edge of the brown paper to the opposite edge. (See illustration.) Draw lines parallel to the first one at one-inch intervals to cover the paper. Erase any lines that come within 1/2 inch of the outer rim of the oval; then use an X-acto® knife to cut on each line. Alternately using yellow, then orange, weave one-inch-wide construction-paper strips through the slits. Trim, adjust, and glue the strips as necessary for a finished look. Top off these tropical treasures by gluing the green cutout to the top of the woven oval. Is that fresh pineapple I smell?

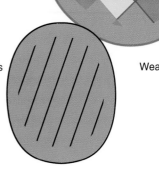

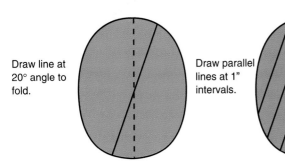

Draw line at 20° angle to fold.

Draw parallel lines at 1" intervals.

Erase lines within 1/2" of rim.

Weave.

Sun Sparklers

Making these colorful sun sparklers is a great creative outlet, but it's also a good way to cut back on unnecessary waste. While you're waiting for laminating film scraps to accumulate, locate several simple illustrations. To make a sun sparkler, draw or trace an illustration onto a scrap of film using permanent or transparency markers. Color the design, and loosely trim around it. Poke a hole near the top of the film, thread with monofilament line, and suspend from a window casing. It's a perky way to brighten your day and lighten the garbage collector's load.

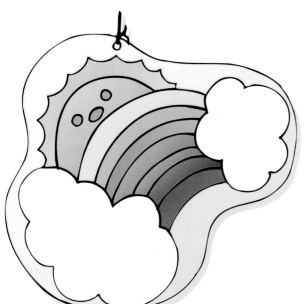

Snip, Snip Art

Get an indispensable art tool into the picture with this unusual abstract art. To begin, trace scissors repeatedly onto a sheet of white art paper, so that the outlines touch and fill the page. Leaving the scissor shapes white, color the spaces around the scissor outlines using three different colors. When the artwork is complete, both fine-motor skills and creativity have had a bit of exercise.

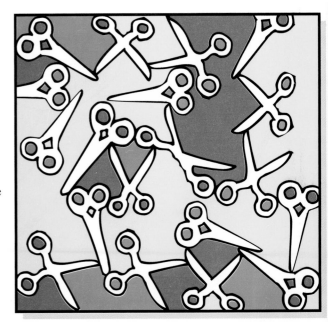

132

fold line

fold line

©The Education Center, Inc.

©The Education Center, Inc.

Anytime

Easy Piñata

Would you like to surprise your students with a piñata, but you don't relish all of the time and mess of making a papier-mâché one? No problem! Just decorate the outside of a shopping bag (the type with handles) with crepe paper, tissue-paper streamers, curling ribbon, balloons, and other festive art materials. Fill the bag with candy and treats; then hang it from the ceiling. There you have it—an instant piñata!

Inside-Out Art

Let imaginations flow with these simple, eye-catching compositions! Glue a rectangular piece of construction paper in the middle of a larger sheet of a contrasting color. Cut out various shapes from the borders of this layered sheet. Glue the remainder of the layered sheet to a larger piece of construction paper. Make sure the construction paper is large enough for the cut-out shapes to be glued to it. Finally glue the shapes to the outside of the borders as shown.

For a variation, cut a magazine picture into a rectangular shape. Cut out shapes along its borders; then glue the remainder of the rectangle to a large sheet of construction paper. Glue the cut-out shapes to the outsides of the borders to look as if they have simply been folded back from the original rectangle.

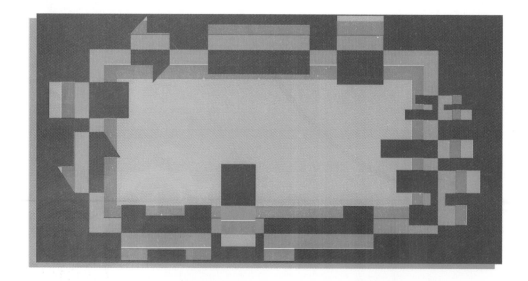

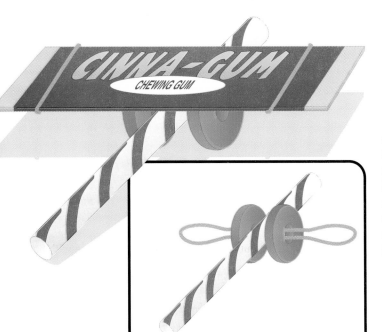

Candy Airplanes

These candy treats are as much fun to make as they are to eat. In preparation for making an airplane, gather two LifeSavers®, one wrapped stick of hard candy, one stick of gum, and one medium-size rubber band. Thread the rubber band through both LifeSavers. Slide the LifeSavers so that one is near each end of the rubber band. Place the stick of candy atop the rubber band as shown. Insert each end of the stick of gum into a rubber band end. Adjust the rubber band for a snug fit. Up, up, and away!

Coffee Bears

Here's a "bear-y" different craft! Save and dry used coffee grounds for this project. Trace a bear-shaped cutout on brown construction paper. Use a permanent marker to draw on a face. If desired, glue on wiggle eyes. Coat the cutout with a thin layer of glue, leaving the face area uncovered. Sprinkle on coffee grounds for the bear's fur. When the glue and grounds are dry, glue on a bow and buttons. Now that's a bear to be proud of!

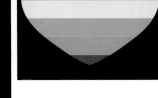

Rainbow Colors

This bright art project is a wonderful follow-up to *A Rainbow Of My Own* by Don Freeman. On art paper, paint strips of color in this order: red, orange, yellow, green, blue, and violet. From a collection of templates, select a favorite design, and trace it onto the dried artwork. Cut out the resulting shape and glue it onto black construction paper.

Anytime ✂

Western Sponge Art

This prickly desert cactus art begins with a soft sponge. Trace a cactus shape onto a sponge; then cut on the outlines. To make a desert scene, dip the sponge into a pan containing a thin layer of green paint. Press the sponge onto old newspapers and then onto a sheet of art paper. Repeat this sponging technique. Allow the paint to dry; then use crayons, markers, or paints to illustrate a desert scene and to add prickly thorns to the cacti.

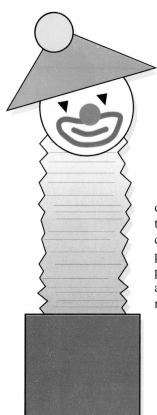

Jack-In-The-Box

Pop up with this geometric jack-in-the-box and your youngsters are sure to cheer! For every other student, you'll need a six-inch paper square. Cut each of these squares in half, creating two triangles. For each student you will need a six-inch paper square, a 4 1/2-inch-diameter paper circle, a 3" x 12" rectangle, and a triangle (from above). Assist students as they glue each of the pieces together as shown to form jack-in-the-boxes. Have each student add a small paper pompom to his jack-in-the-box's hat. To be certain "Jack" will pop from his box, assist students in accordion-folding the rectangular pieces. Have students draw facial features on the circles using markers. Display these pop-up toy cutouts together to create your own classroom Toyland.

Circle Pictures

Don't toss those tubes! Use cardboard tubes from bathroom tissue, paper towels, or wrapping paper for this art project. Cut each tube into several sections. Provide art paper and several colors of tempera paint.

Students dunk cardboard tube pieces in paint and press onto their papers to create unusual creatures. Features may be added with crayons or markers.

Blot Pictures

Here's a great color exploration activity that creates vivid abstract art. Fold a piece of art paper in half. Open the paper and drizzle glue generously on one half of the paper. Drop two drops each of red, yellow, and blue food coloring onto the glue. Refold the paper and rub very gently to flatten. Unfold the paper again, and allow for drying time. This vivid artwork will make a striking collection when all of your students' projects are displayed together.

An alternative for displaying these projects is to have students cut the dried artwork into various shapes and incorporate them into seasonal art projects.

Cathedral Windows

Allow the beauty of stained glass windows to fill your classroom with streams of vivid colors. To make a window, paint two-inch squares of several colors of tissue paper onto a piece of waxed paper using watered-down glue. Overlap the tissue paper if necessary to completely cover the waxed paper. When the glue is dry, glue a black construction-paper frame to each side. Trim away the excess waxed paper and tape to your classroom windows.

Designer Dinos

Dinosaurs are always a hot topic. So encourage your youngsters to get creative about dinosaurs. To make a designer dinosaur, begin by drawing a large dinosaur shape on a sheet of construction paper. Cut out the design and glue it to a sheet of black construction paper. (Another alternative is to sponge-print a dinosaur shape onto the black paper, rather than gluing it.) Use cotton balls, yarn, colored sand, glitter, paint pens, colored pasta, tissue paper, aquarium rocks, and colored popcorn to make your dinosaur distinctively different. Looks like it's time for a private showing. The dino designs are complete!

Anytime

Class Baby Blanket

Teach your students the basics of sewing and the pride of giving with this unique class project.

Materials:

fabric squares (one per child)   fabric crayons
gingham strips   iron
cotton batting   backing material
yarn   sewing machine
needles   thread
pins   scissors

Steps:

1. Have each student decorate his square with fabric crayons.
2. Set drawings with iron as directed on package of fabric crayons.
3. Sew squares together with gingham strips on sewing machine.
4. Sandwich batting between backing material and sewn squares.
5. Pin layers together.
6. Have students sew and tie layers together with yarn lengths in comforter fashion.
7. Have students sew edges together with needle and thread.
8. When finished, donate blanket to local charity.

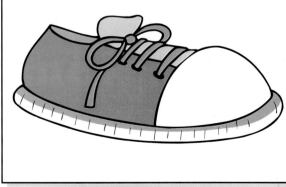

Fancy Footwork

You won't have to sneak up on your youngsters to create a sensation with this sneaker art. Capitalize on the popularity of footwear fashions by having students use their sneakers as still life. Have each student remove one of his shoes, place it on his desktop, and sketch it on art paper. Encourage students to use as much detail as possible in their drawings. Provide markers, watercolor paints and brushes, colored pencils, or crayons for completing the artwork. Now that's fancy footwork!

What A Catch!

Here's an art project youngsters will fall for hook, line, and sinker. To make a fish for your stringer, trace a fish shape onto a large sheet of art paper, and cut it out. Use a ruler to draw an assortment of lines; then color each resulting space a bright, cheery color. Glue on foil fins and a button eye for a fishy finish. To display your classroom catch, connect the fish cutouts to a crepe-paper "stringer." Ah-h-h, the fish are biting today!

Coat-Hanger Clown

When you propose this clown artwork, grins and giggles are certain to appear. Trim a six-inch, white construction-paper square to create a circle. Then decorate the circle as a clown's face. Decorate a triangle as his hat, and glue it atop the face. Tape the face to the hook of a coat hanger which has been stretched into a diamond shape. On a folded piece of construction paper, trace the outline of your hand. Cut through both thicknesses, and tape a hand cutout to each side of the hanger. Trace your shoe print onto a folded piece of construction paper. Cut through both pieces and tape these cutouts to the bottom of the hanger to complete the clown.

Sea Creature Pop-Ups

Dive into this three-dimensional art activity. To make a pop-up, first select and find out about a sea creature of your choice and his habitat. Then cut two 2 1/2" slits one inch apart in the center of a 5" x 8" index card. Fold the card in half; then unfold it again. On the half of the card above the fold line, draw your sea creature's habitat. On the other half, draw the ocean floor and write the name of the sea creature. Fold the card to a 90° angle. Press between the slits to push the strip forward. Crease the strip to form a right angle with the card. On a 2 1/2-inch white paper square, draw and color your sea creature; then cut loosely around its form. Glue the back of this cutout to the protruding strip of the folded index card. C-o-o-o-l! You've just created a three-dimensional ocean scene!

To combine several of these scenes into a booklet, fold each scene flat. Then stack them one atop the other. Glue adjacent cards together. Fold a six-inch-wide tagboard strip for covers; then glue it to the top and bottom index cards. You can bet this student-created, pop-up book will be a popular addition to your classroom library!

sea horse

Anytime

Mosaic Masterpieces

These colorful, mosaic creations would make Picasso pause for a moment of admiration! In advance, have students cut the colors from paint sample cards into irregular-shaped pieces, then sort by colors into small containers. Each student draws an outline sketch on a piece of poster board. To create a mosaic, he "paints" his picture by gluing individual paint pieces to his drawing. To achieve a glossy finish, apply Mod Podge® to completed projects or spray (in a well-ventilated area) with an acrylic spray coating.

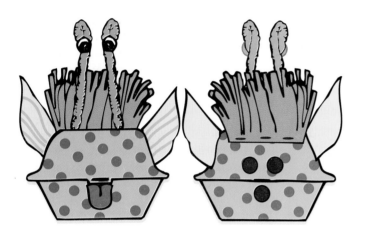

Positively Puppets

With puppets, anything is possible! Mix a small amount of liquid dish detergent into assorted colors of liquid tempera paint; then paint the outer surface of a Styrofoam® sandwich container. (The liquid detergent helps the paint adhere to the Styrofoam surface.) Use an X-acto® knife to cut three small circles in the back of the container as shown. Personalize the container by decorating it with an assortment of art supplies such as construction-paper scraps, felt or material scraps, yarn, ribbon, buttons, glitter, cotton balls, and wiggle eyes. When the time is right, place the fingers and thumb of one hand in the holes at the back of the puppet and bring the puppet to life! Students will have loads of fun role-playing and performing skits with their new puppet creations!

Native American Art

Native Americans recorded important tribal events by painting symbols on animal skins. Your youngsters can simulate this type of communication using brown paper bags, paint, and/or potato prints. Select Native American symbols from a reference book to share with your youngsters. Repeatedly wad up a large piece of brown paper bag which has been torn to resemble an animal skin. Then spread the paper out on a flat surface. Using bright colors of paint such as red, yellow, and orange, paint or potato-print the symbols of your choice onto the paper. These imitation animal skins make a striking and intriguing display to complement your Native American studies.

A Tree For All Seasons

Branch out with these "tree-mendously" appealing art projects. Students can complete each project during the appropriate season, or they can complete all four projects as they study the seasons. Each project is completed on a 6" x 9" piece of construction paper; then it is mounted atop a slightly larger construction-paper rectangle.

Fall Tree: For fall foliage, load each of several cotton balls with fall-colored chalkdust—one color per cotton ball. To do this rub each cotton ball along the side of a chubby stick of chalk. Then dab and smear the colors together to create the desired effect. Use a similar technique to make the tree trunk.

Spring Tree: For a blossom-filled tree, clip a piece of sponge to each of three clothespins. Pour a small amount of brown, white, and pink tempera paint into separate containers. First sponge-print the brown tree trunk and branches. When the paint has dried, print a flurry of pink and white blossoms.

Winter Tree: To begin, attach strips of thin masking tape to white construction paper to create the shape of a barren winter tree. Using watercolors and a wide brush, paint the entire surface of the project. When the paint has dried, carefully remove the masking-tape strips.

Summer Tree: To create this greenery, cut a supply of tiny tissue-paper squares. Lightly coat the top half of the paper with thinned glue. Arrange the tissue paper as desired; then brush a second coat of thinned glue over the tissue-paper arrangement. For the tree trunk, glue overlapping pieces of torn, brown construction paper in place.

Anytime ✂️🖍️

Wrapping Paper

Here is a simple way to make colorful and unique wrapping paper. First fold a sheet of white tissue paper, accordion-style, to a width of two inches. Beginning at one end of the folded paper, fold as you would a flag, making triangles with each fold. After the last fold, you will have one thick triangle. Dip each corner in water and then in different colors of food coloring. Allow to dry overnight, since the paper tears easily when wet. Unfold. Each sheet will be colorful, different, and ready to use!

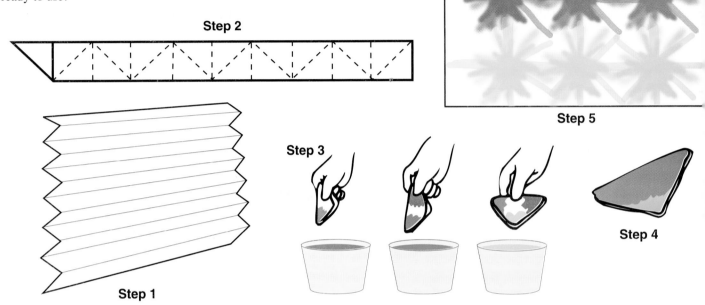

Step 2

Step 5

Step 3

Step 4

Step 1

Luminous And Lovely

Create luminous spring works of art with the help of a simple cooking ingredient. Give each student a 12" x 18" piece of white drawing paper. On the paper, have the student use a pencil to very lightly draw a simple, large flower or flower arrangement. Provide watercolors for students to paint their sketches. Instruct students to use lots of water so that the paint appears light in most areas. After the painting has dried completely, turn it over on a few sheets of newspaper. Rub the back of the painting with a crumpled paper towel that has been soaked with cooking oil. When an area has soaked up the oil and looks wet, move on to another area until the entire paper is oiled. Let the oiled paintings dry overnight; then rub the backs of them with a clean paper towel to remove any excess oil. The finished paintings will appear transparent, so be sure to display them on your classroom windows.

COOKING OIL

Magazine Abstract

Need a simple art activity for a Friday afternoon? Look no further!

Steps:

1. Cut out a full-page, color picture from a magazine.
2. Using a ruler and pencil, divide the back of the picture into equal vertical strips.
3. Number the strips; then cut them apart.
4. Glue the first strip on a piece of background paper, being sure that the top of the strip is aligned with the top of the paper.
5. Glue the second strip beside the first strip but about 1/2" lower on the paper.
6. Glue the remaining strips in order as shown.
7. Trim the background paper along the bottom edge of the lowered strips.

Ping-Pong® Paintings

Have a ball! A Ping-Pong ball, that is. To create this abstract artwork, begin by mixing two tablespoons of paint with one tablespoon of water in a cup. Similarly prepare another cup with a contrasting color of paint. Place a Ping-Pong ball in each cup and stir with craft sticks until each ball is coated with paint. In a gift box lid, place a piece of paper and one Ping-Pong ball. Repeatedly tilt the lid back and forth, causing the ball to leave trails of paint on the paper. Replace this ball with the other one to create contrasting trails. When the paint trails are dry, glue the paper to a sheet of construction paper for display.

Anytime

The tired, red sun sets down to rest for the dark hours and all through the night.

Haiku Art

To motivate students to write poetry with feeling and expression, try this art project first. Have each child splash paint droplets onto a 9" x 6" piece of white construction paper. The student then blows through a drinking straw to spread the paint into unique patterns. Next have children write haiku poems based on themes of nature and beauty. Have each student cut out his poem and glue it to the colorful background to create a beautiful frame.

Shape Art

Simple, overlapping shapes produce striking results with a trace-and-color technique. Each child draws a shape on heavy paper and cuts it out. The student then makes several overlapping tracings of his shape on white art paper, drawing them at various angles. To complete the project, the student colors the individual parts of his shapes so that no two parts of the same color are side by side. Mount the completed project onto construction paper of a contrasting color.

"FAN-tastic" Art

Have "fan-tastic" fun with this simple art activity. Fold a sheet of construction paper (9" x 6") accordion-style to create a fan. Pinch and twist one end. Glue or staple the fan to art paper in any position. Use your imagination to make a drawing using the fan as part of the picture. Then use crayons or markers to add color.

Fancy Fireworks!

This creative writing/art project is a wonderful summer school activity or anytime-of-the-year project. First have students write descriptive paragraphs about fireworks, including their personal experiences and feelings, as well as descriptions about the sounds and colors of fireworks. After talking and writing about fireworks, have students create their own! Follow these steps:

1. Trim a sheet of white paper so that it will fit in the bottom of a gift box. (A shirt box is a good size.)
2. Put two or three drops of different colors of paint on the paper.
3. Place two or three marbles in the box.
4. Put the lid on the box.
5. Shake and slide the box back and forth.
6. Take the lid off the box and sprinkle the paint with glitter.
7. Remove the sheet of paper and let it dry.
8. Attach the writing to the bottom of the picture.

A Patchwork Quilt

Making a classroom patchwork quilt is a fun way for students to creatively share their personal interests and discover the interests of their classmates. Show students a patchwork quilt before beginning the project. Have each student personalize and decorate an eight-inch construction-paper or tagboard square to represent his special interests. Punch holes at even intervals along all four sides of each completed square (making certain the holes are in the same location on each square). Loosely lace the quilt squares together using yarn. Display the completed quilt on a paper-cover bulletin board. Encourage students to explain the details of their squares to their classmates.

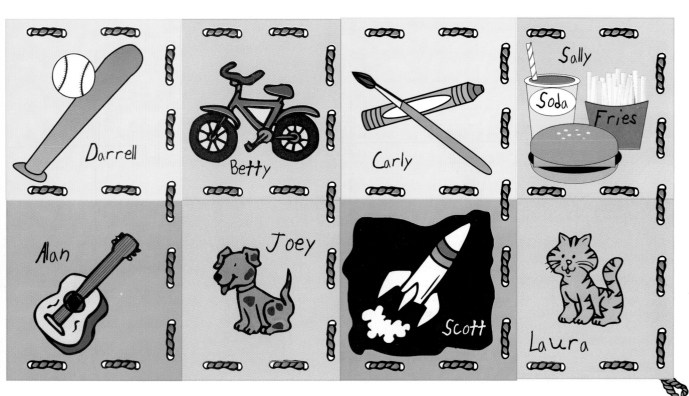

145

Anytime

From Bottle To Beast

Creative juices will bubble over when students make these bottle beasts! Collect a variety of plastic bottles such as those used for glue, liquid detergent, and shampoo. Be sure that the bottles have been rinsed out thoroughly; then cover them with papier-mâché. After the papier-mâché has completely dried, paint the bottles with bright tempera paint. Use bottle caps, felt, buttons, and other scrap materials for the finishing touches such as eyes, mouths, teeth, etc. To make each beast's feet, cut two small Styrofoam® balls in half and paint them. When dry, glue the feet to the beast. Have students write creative stories about their beastly creations; then display the creatures in a menagerie that's sure to be an attention-grabber!

May I Have A Letter?

Need a quick and easy art project for a Friday afternoon? Then give new life to old bulletin-board letters! Give one letter to each student. Challenge the student to glue the letter in any position on a piece of art paper. The student then uses crayons or markers to draw a picture incorporating the letter in a unique way. What a fun way to stretch your students' imaginations!

Rag Rug

If your class is studying colonial life or you're looking for a cooperative art project, let students make a rag rug. Cut a large number of fabric strips, approximately 1 1/2" to 2" wide. Have students tie or hand-stitch the strips end to end, making three very long strips. Students then braid the strips together until a desired length is achieved. Coil the braid and have students stitch the rug together. This worthwhile project can be time-consuming, so allow students to work on it during free time throughout the year.

It's Raining, It's Pouring!

A cold, rainy day is the perfect time for students to create their own wet weather scenes. Have each student draw a picture of a rainstorm scene, coloring it with crayons. To add realistic "raindrops," have the child make short slashes on his paper with a blue or purple, nonpermanent marker. Fill a sink or bucket with water. Instruct each student to dip his picture in the water, making sure the rain "falls" in a downward direction. After drying, display these pictures on a bulletin board or hang them on a clothesline suspended across the classroom.

Anytime

Precious Piglets

Not since Wilbur of *Charlotte's Web* fame has there been a piglet this precious! And wouldn't this art project make a wonderful follow-up activity to a reading of E. B. White's classic? To begin, inflate a round balloon to a diameter of approximately six inches. Then use newspaper and wallpaper paste to cover the entire balloon in papier-mâché. Once the paper and paste have dried, glue on a plastic ice-cream cup for the snout and four halved toilet-tissue tubes for legs. (To speed up this process, you may want to attach these pieces for the children using a hot glue gun.) Use more newspaper and wallpaper paste to papier-mâché the snout and legs. When this is dry, paint the piglet. Finish the piglet by attaching felt ears, button eyes, bead nostrils, and a spiraled pipe-cleaner tail. Now *that's* a fine swine!

Bubble Prints

Prints from bubbles make an unusual art activity—and lots of warm weather fun when the projects are completed outdoors! In a bowl, combine tempera paint with a small amount of liquid detergent. Using a straw, blow into the mixture until bubbles extend over the rim of the bowl. Quickly place a sheet of white construction paper over the top of the bowl; then remove the paper and let the resulting "bubble print" dry. For double bubble fun, repeat the procedure several times using differently sized bowls and a variety of paint colors. Mount the completed projects atop slightly larger sheets of colored construction paper.

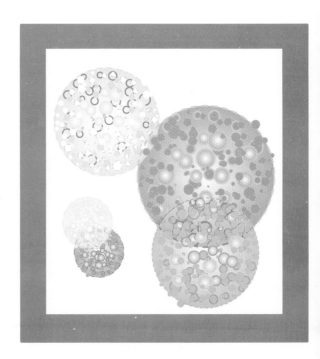

Paper-Bag Frogs

Have children create a pond full of croakers for a 3-D bulletin board.

Materials needed for each child:

small lunch bag   newspapers
tagboard
tagboard leg pattern (see illustration)
green and light green tempera paint
scraps of green, black, white, and pink construction
     paper
craft glue, pencil, scissors, stapler, paintbrushes

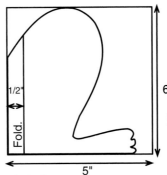

Steps:

1. Stuff the bag with newspapers. Fold the top down and staple.
2. Trace the leg pattern twice onto tagboard and cut out. Cut out three circles from tagboard, each three inches in diameter.
3. Paint the entire bag green. Paint one of the tagboard circles and both of the leg cutouts green on both sides. Allow to dry. Then paint light green spots over the green.
4. Cut the painted circle in half and glue each half to one of the remaining circles to make eyes and eyelids. Cut an iris, pupil, and lashes for each eye from paper scraps. Glue eyes to the paper bag.
5. Fold back 1/2 inch on the insides of legs. Put glue on fold of each leg and hold against the bag as shown until glue adheres.
6. Curl a 1/2-inch-wide piece of pink construction paper around a pencil and glue to body as shown for the tongue.

"Sunsations"

Fill your windows with sunshine with this "sunsational" art project. The stained-glass effect will brighten your whole classroom with warm colors.

Materials needed for each child:

10" circle of waxed paper
6" circle and additional scraps of black construction paper
scraps of red, yellow, orange, gold, pink, and purple tissue paper
white glue
scissors

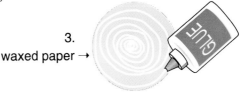

3.
waxed paper →

Steps:

1. Fold black circle in half.
2. Cut out the inside to make a circular frame. Cut out rays, eyes, and smile from the construction-paper scraps.
3. Squeeze a thin line of glue in a spiral from the center of the waxed paper outward. Position black circular frame, rays, and features on the waxed paper to make a smiling sun as shown.
4. Place pieces of tissue paper over the construction-paper sun, overlapping different colors and covering the waxed paper completely.
5. Dry overnight and peel off the waxed paper.
6. Hang "sunsations" in windows for a stained-glass effect.

Anytime ✂️

Sensational Still Lifes

Create still life masterpieces with an art lesson that combines media. Place a few still life objects (vase, fruit, book, etc.) on a table in a corner of your room. Schedule small groups of students to visit the area at one time. Have each student draw a picture of the still life on a 12" x 18" piece of tagboard or poster board. Instruct students to draw large and start drawing two to three inches from the bottom of the paper. After the drawing is completed, have the student add a horizontal line behind the objects to create the appearance of a table or other surface.

After all drawings are completed, have students paint their pictures with tempera paint, painting each area a solid color. Let the paintings dry completely; then have students use colorful chalk to add designs on the still life objects, the table, and the background. Encourage students to use patterns and repetitive designs. Spray finished pictures with a fixative to prevent smearing. The results will be worth framing!

A "Value-able" Art Lesson

Give your students a lesson in *value* (the relative lightness or darkness of a color) with this fun project.

Steps:

1. Draw several curvy or zigzagged, horizontal lines on a piece of white art paper.
2. Prepare a small container of white paint.
3. Add three or four drops of dark-colored paint to the white and mix. Paint this color on the top section of your paper.
4. Add three or four more drops of the dark paint to the mixture. Mix; then paint the second section.
5. Continue in this manner, painting each section a slightly darker color as you move down the paper. Let dry.
6. On construction paper, draw a simple object such as an animal, house, tree, etc. Cut it out.
7. On construction paper, draw the same object in a medium size and a smaller size. Cut them out.
8. Glue the largest cut-out object closest to the bottom of your paper. Glue the medium-sized object higher up and the smallest object even higher.

"Pointed" Paintings

Introduce your students to the art technique known as *pointillism.* A picture using this method is composed of dots and specks. When viewed from afar, the picture may appear to look like a solid mass of color.

Create your own pointillism pictures using various colors of paint; a new, sharpened pencil for each color of paint; and a piece of paper. Draw a simple picture with a dotted outline lightly in pencil. Dip the erasers and points of the pencils in paint; then stamp them on your paper to cover the pencil dot outline. Let dry. Surprise—if you look at the picture and squint, the colors may appear to move!

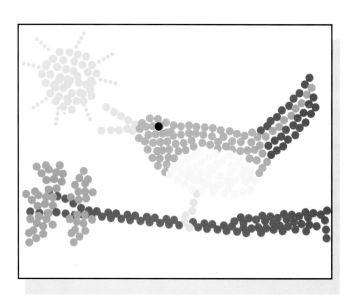

Group Murals

Your students will enjoy the results of this cooperative art project. Divide students into groups of six to eight. Give each group a greeting-card picture that has been cut into strips, one per child. Each student takes a strip and a large piece of drawing paper that has been cut to the same proportion as the card strip. He then attempts to reproduce his card strip's artwork on his larger piece of paper. Have each group put its completed sections together (the finished sections won't match exactly). The result: several interesting murals that will turn quite a few heads!

Anytime ✂️

Geometric Patterns

Give students a lesson on analogous and complementary color with a creative cut-paper project. To prepare, use a paper cutter and cut a large supply of 1 1/2" construction-paper squares in a variety of colors. Give each student a 9" x 9" piece of construction paper and glue. Review *analogous* (similar) *colors* such as blue and green or red and orange. Have each student choose two analogous colors; then have him glue those colors of squares on his paper in a six by six grid to create a symmetrical pattern.

Next discuss *complementary colors* (colors that are opposite one another on the color wheel, such as red and green or orange and blue). Have each student choose a third color of square, one that complements a color on his grid. The student cuts these squares into various shapes and glues them in a symmetrical pattern on the grid. Mount finished designs on large sheets of white paper; then mount them on a contrasting sheet of paper. The results are stunning!

Foil Sculptures

With a twist here and a scrunch there, your students can turn aluminum foil into lifelike sculptures! Cut a large square of aluminum foil in three places as shown. Scrunch the top left and right sections to make arms. Mold the head from the middle section. Wrinkle the bottom two halves to make legs. Continue molding until your sculpture is doing something that you enjoy doing—dancing, playing tennis, etc. Make additional props out of construction paper and other materials; then glue them to your sculpture. Finally tape or glue the feet of your model to a small square of poster board. Group your students' models together for a display that's sure to be the center of attention!

Edible Peanut-Butter Clay

Try this recipe for an afternoon of modeling fun and a tasty snack all in one! Mix 2 cups of peanut butter with 1 cup of honey. (Swirl 1 teaspoon of oil in the measuring cup before measuring to avoid sticking.) Add 3 cups of instant dry milk, a little at a time, until stiff. Blend with hands. Refrigerate overnight. The next day, provide each child with a piece of waxed paper and some peanut-butter clay. Have students mold their clay into different shapes. When finished, let the students eat their creations. This recipe makes enough clay for 18 students.)

Paper Sculpture

This is a great art project that requires little preparation time on your part! For each student, provide a sheet of 9" x 12" construction paper, glue, and scissors. Students tear, bend, fold, cut, or roll the paper in any way they wish. If a piece is cut off, the student must glue it back somewhere on the project. Your students will have fun creating anything from a lion's mask to a skateboard course complete with skateboards!

Buttermilk Art

Kids may not be eager to drink buttermilk, but did they know they can paint with it? Paint a porous, soft (rather than stiff) piece of paper with a thin layer of buttermilk. Let the buttermilk dry almost completely; then draw on it using a soft chalk pastel or an oil-based chalk. The finished product will resemble an oil painting. Your kids will love this strange medium!

Anytime

Easy Dye

Here's a quick and easy way to dye macaroni, rice, beans, and seeds for art projects. In individual containers, pour a small amount of rubbing alcohol and tint to desired shades with food coloring. Drop the objects to be dyed into the liquid, let sit a minute, and then spoon out onto waxed paper. The alcohol evaporates quickly, leaving dyed objects ready for art.

Wall Plaques

Students will be pleased to take home these easy-to-make wall plaque

For each wall plaque you will need:

tile	ultrafine glitter
picture from a greeting card	12" of ribbon, two inches wide
Mod Podge®	1 1/4" metal ring
scissors	glue
	paintbrush

Have each student cut out his greeting-card picture. Next the student paints Mod Podge onto his tile and lays the cutout on top, pressing down on the picture to assure that it is firmly attached. Let dry for 15 to 20 minutes. Repeat this step, letting each layer of Mod Podge dry, until desired finish is achieved. Before the final coat is dry, sprinkle with diamond dust and shake off the excess. Slide the metal ring onto the ribbon and fold ribbon in half. Glue the ribbon ends together and let dry. When dry, glue the ribbon to the plaque to create a hanger.

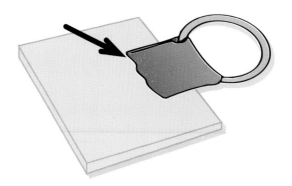

The Hippest Hippos

Each of your students will be convinced that this hippo is the hippest—and he'll be correct. Provide art paper and pencils; then call out and demonstrate the step-by-step directions below for drawing a hippo.

Steps:

1. In the middle of your paper, draw a large circle for the hippo's body.
2. In the middle of the large circle, draw a small circle for the hippo's muzzle.
3. Near the bottom of the muzzle, draw a half-circle smile and draw half-circles at both ends of the smile.
4. Near the top of the small circle, draw two half-circles for nostrils. Put a dot under each nostril.
5. Atop the muzzle, draw a half-oval for the rest of the hippo's head.
6. Near the top of the hippo's head, draw two circles for eyes. Put a dot in each eye.
7. Atop the hippo's head, draw two half-circles for ears.
8. Near the bottom of the large circle that is the hippo's body, draw four half-circles for feet. Then put three tiny circles in each half-circle to complete the feet.

Suggest that your youngsters let their imaginations run wild as they color their beasts in the hippest of colors.

Spectacular Shapes

Watch abstract artwork take shape before your very eyes with this nifty project. Cut each of the following shapes from a different color of construction paper: square, rectangle, circle, equilateral triangle. To begin, fold the square cutout in half. Then, cutting into the fold, cut a slightly smaller shape from the folded paper. Continue in this manner until the center of the fold is reached. Unfold the resulting shapes and set them aside. Repeat this entire procedure with each of the remaining cutouts. Then glue the collection of shapely cutouts on a 9" x 12" sheet of black construction paper in an overlapping fashion. Colorful and spectacular!

Anytime ✂🖍

Larger-Than-Life Cartooning

Convert your classroom into Cartoon Town for an art class with surprising results. Enlarge or reduce a colorful cartoon or coloring-book scene to three inches square. (You will need one scene for every nine children in your class.) Draw a one-inch grid over the scene, and cut on the lines. Distribute these pieces at random to students. On a six-inch paper square, instruct each student to precisely enlarge his design to match and color. Youngsters will be fascinated with the results when the completed squares are positioned to reveal the picture.

Weed Pocket

Tuck some dried weeds into paper pockets to emphasize nature's autumn artistry. Begin by collecting dried weeds for the project. Then snip the sides of a u-shaped construction-paper pocket as shown. Decorate the pocket using markers or crayons. Glue it to a contrasting sheet of construction paper, being certain to leave the pocket open at the top. Tape a bouquet of weeds at the stems and tuck them inside the pocket. Display these weed pockets side by side on a bulletin board or in a hallway for maximum impact.

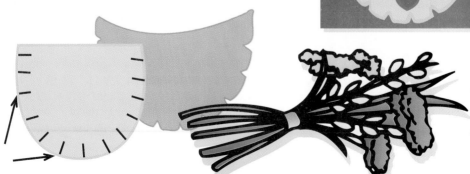

Paper Gardens

Introduce your students to the following techniques to make unique 3-D pieces for a flower garden collage. Ask students to bring various scraps of wrapping paper from home. Provide a variety of colors of construction paper, scissors, glue, and tape. Then let the fun begin!

- Accordion-fold a 4" x 6" piece of colorful paper. Pinch one end together and glue a strip of paper around the end to hold it in place (see illustration). Create a variety of flowers by using different types of paper of various sizes.

- Cut a long strip of colorful paper. Make cuts along the length as shown. Roll up the paper and secure it with a piece of tape or with glue. Bend the petals back. Add leaves and a stem. For a variation, glue two contrasting colors of paper strips back-to-back. Then follow the steps above to create a flower. Vary the widths of the cuts, make the cuts pointed or rounded, or bend back alternating strips to make lots of different flowers.

- To make a stem, cut a paper straw into shorter pieces. Wrap a thin strip of green paper around one of the pieces of straw. Glue or tape the ends.

- Cut out different shapes for various types of leaves: long and thin, short and pointed. Score down the middle of the leaf, and fold. Leaves can be used to cover up the joint between a flower and its stem.

- Cut several petals of different sizes from various colors of paper. Place the largest petals on the paper first, positioning them before gluing. Place another layer of petals on the first layer and glue (see illustration). Continue overlapping and gluing several layers. Add green sepals around the bottom of the flower. Make curls above the flower by wrapping narrow strips of paper around a pencil.

Paper Towel Art

Turn a simple paper towel into an eye-catching art project. Provide each student with a sturdy paper towel, one that has a floral or other design. Have the student color in the designs with crayons, then outline the designs with a black crayon or permanent marker. (If using permanent markers, remind students to place newspaper underneath their paper towels.) Next submerge each towel in water, remove it, and squeeze out the excess water. Carefully spread out the towel on a layer of paper. While the towel is wet, use a paintbrush to dab one watercolor around the designs on the towel. Since the towel is wet, the paint will spread to make an attractive background for the designs.

Index

Index continued...

Index continued...